Attention to Detail

I0600079

To Teddy Mass of I. Mass and Sons, a building contractor who became my friend while teaching me how to build a house with love.

Attention to Detail

Herbert H. Wise

Studio photography by David Frazier
Research by Emelie Tolley

TH
2025
W57

New York   London   Tokyo

Copyright © Quick Fox, 1979
All rights reserved.

International Standard Book Number:
0-8256-3174-2 (hard cover)
0-8256-3171-8 (paperback)

Library of Congress Catalog Card Number: 79-65942
Printed in Japan.

No part of this book may be reproduced or transmitted in any
form or by any means, electronic or mechanical, including
photocopying, without permission in writing from the pub-
lisher: Quick Fox, 33 West 60th Street, New York 10023.

In Great Britain:
Book Sales Ltd., 78 Newman Street, London W1P 3LA.

In Canada:
Gage Trade Publishing, P.O. Box 5000, 164 Commander Blvd.,
Agincourt, Ontario M1S 3C7.

In Japan:
Quick Fox, 4-26-22 Jingumae, Shibuya-ku, Tokyo 150.

In Germany:
Music Sales Gmbh, Kölner Strasse 199, D-5000 Cologne 90,
West Germany.

Design: Joseph L. Santoro
Additional written text: Julia Kagan
Locations: Jamie Simpson
Cover: Dennis Mortensen, architect

Contents

Introduction

Some years ago a very good friend decided to pull up stakes and leave New York. There wasn't, he claimed, a decent home to be had in all of Manhattan. It was my pleasure to prove him wrong. At the critical moment, I discovered just the type of place he had convinced himself did not exist: a magnificient Victorian brownstone, a glorious townhouse on a lush, tree-lined block — and it was for sale. To be sure, the place needed a good deal of work. The house had gone to seed. But the proportions of the rooms were marvelous. With work and imagination, the possibilities were endless and exciting. And the price, even for a person with his bags packed and his eye on the wide open spaces of suburbia, was more than right. One look and my friend was convinced. He would take it.

As so often happens in the spirit of such moments, people say things or make promises with perfect sincerity that they later live to regret. And I, caught up in my own enthusiasm for seeing my "find" restored to its former glory, was guilty of committing just such an act. Anticipating the thrill of installing new doors, of selecting new molding, of re-building the kitchen from floor to overhead cabinets and the bathroom from toilet to tub, I heard myself blurt out: "And leave the renovations to me."

The regret, although it was not apparent at the time, turned out to be painfully simple: the house was not mine. Ultimately, I was not the one who had to be satisfied with the final result. It was a hard lesson. I had already lived through the renovation of my own house years before. And I remembered loving every minute — getting involved in everything, participating, seeing the rooms evolve from little more than empty shells into fully realized living and working environments that reflected my personal needs and aesthetic concerns — watching my house become my home.

What I did *not* remember was how I had made the myriad decisions concerning doors, hinges, knobs, frames, countertops, sinks, faucets, floor tiles, toilets, switch plates, balusters and a hundred other architectural details more or less by instinct. I did not sit down with an enormously thick book of alternatives and flip through the pages, pondering options at my leisure; no such volume existed. I might have written to the various manufacturers for information about this or that, but I didn't know who they were or what they made. I certainly was not conscious of the bewildering variety of choices available for practically every minute aspect of one's home. However, I was lucky. I knew exactly what I wanted item by item. I gave my contractor precise descriptions of everything and what he couldn't locate, I did. Whatever design sense had to be accommodated, whatever practicalities had to be taken into account, began and ended with a single individual: me.

Now I was involved in something quite different. I was renovating someone else's house. And in trying to restore it to sparkling condition, again I was faced with countless choices of a purely personal nature, but I was not the person to make them. *My* instincts, here, didn't count one whit. And to complicate things even more, the instincts of my friend and his wife were not parallel to my own.

For example, consider the kitchen. Should it have a porcelain sink or a stainless steel sink? Each has its own set of pluses and minuses. To me the choice was obvious, and automatic. But I kept my mouth shut. Instead I said to the lady of the house: "What kind of sink would you like?" She gave me a slightly puzzled look. She hadn't, I suspect, anticipated a question of that sort. She simply thought these things were just *done*.

I tried a different tack. "We're building the kitchen over again," I said. "We're putting in a new countertop. It could be made of almost anything; Corian, stainless steel, marble, granite, slate, butcher block. It could be a hard wood, or masonite, or linoleum, or mosaic tile. But before you simply close your eyes and make a choice, consider the options with regard to the sink. What kind of sink would you like to go into what kind of countertop?"

In the house of her childhood there had been an old white porcelain sink. The recollection was pleasant. The idea of having a porcelain sink *now* came into her mind.

Now, porcelain sinks are fine. But I could see that she was new at this. "There are," I said, "certain disadvantages to porcelain sinks. For one thing, they tend to cost more than other kinds. And they come in fewer styles, for porcelain is a very difficult material to shape. Porcelain is not especially durable. So, if you drop a heavy pot in a porcelain sink, likely as not it will crack or chip."

This only seemed to confuse things. I was trying to make her understand that you don't *just* put in a sink, *any* sink. That's a one-way route to disappointment. The choice must be intelligent and informed, based on your particular preferences and needs.

She asked about the alternatives, so I told her something about stainless steel sinks. They are, for example, less expensive than porcelain sinks — that is a plus. But they tend to look messy, spotted. You can run water in a stainless steel sink, dry the basin thoroughly

with a towel and it will look clean. But draw a simple glass of water from the tap and the messy look returns. That is a characteristic of stainless steel. On the other hand, there are distinct advantages to that material. Because it is an easy material to shape, stainless steel sinks are available in a variety of styles: round, square, oblong, two-compartment, three-compartment and many more. You can order a special compartment for a garbage disposal, a food processor, or a blender. You can get one high compartment for preparing food and a deeper one for dishwashing. The range of alternatives is spectacular. But the right combination of choices can only be determined by you.

And so we went, my friend and I, step by step, through all the options concerning architectural details for each room in the house. Once we had settled on a countertop and a sink, there was a staggering array of faucets to consider. Should there be a single-lever faucet or double valves? Should there be a high spout or a low one? What about a filter spray? Or an automatic soap dispenser? Or a boiling water spigot for coffee and tea?

By the time we had answered each of these questions for every room in the house, I had undergone an important expansion of consciousness. I came to realize something that hadn't sunk in when I was restoring my own house, guided purely by instinct: that the range of choices to be considered for each aspect of architectural detail was truly overwhelming. Moreover, it was paramount to have some conception of that range, for collectively those details, major and minor, become the sum and substance of your home, contributing to the sense of pleasure and comfort you derive — or lack of it.

There was, however, a small obstacle to this high ideal. The wealth of choices, tremendous though it was, remained like an iceberg, largely hidden from the public eye. Developing a sense of the scope of items available, category by category, was, for the novice, next to impossible. There might be an odd brochure here and another one there, but they tended to focus on a specific item. The view they gave was strictly limited. Frequently they were not readily available and were time-consuming to collect. Ultimately, they left serious gaps in the consciousness of even the most indefatigable of renovators. Clearly, the need existed for something more comprehensive, something to guide a homeowner's thinking, to give it direction, definition, and focus so that the best personal choices might be found. That is how the idea for *Attention to Detail* was born.

Attention to Detail, while catalog-like in some respects, is not meant to be the last word on its subject.

In these pages you will not find every floor covering on the market, or every molding pattern available, or every *anything* for that matter. The sole purpose of the book, in a colorful, vibrant and attractive way, is to expand your consciousness, to open your eyes to the scope, the range, the rich variety of alternatives available in each important area of architectural detail. It offers you an opportunity to consider these variables systematically in each room of your house. It provides you with a framework for specifying your needs to a contractor, for saying, in effect: "I know you told me you were going to put a new countertop in here. Now here is the kind of countertop I want." Leave it to the contractor to guess what you want and he will, without a doubt, guess wrong.

To this end, almost 1,000 items are described or illustrated in color. Each item, even if it is manufactured abroad, is readily available here in the U.S. Each photograph is numerically keyed into a special appendix in the back of the volume where the names and addresses of the various manufacturers are listed. Most of the items illustrated are built-in rather than applied or tacked on; that is, they involve architectural and design considerations more than the cosmetic and transitory ones of interior decoration. There are a few applied items such as moldings and lighting switchplates because it was felt that they are more architectural than decorative in character.

There are two kinds of photographic presentation. The first is catalog-like to give you an overview of styles and the colors of a particular item at a glance. These photographs were sometimes supplied by the manufacturer but more often we obtained the actual item and did the photographing ourselves. The second form of presentation consists of photographs taken "in the field." They depict how many of the items fit into some truly superb homes throughout the country—and how they each contribute to the overall effect. The entire range of items available of a certain type could not possibly be included. We had to be selective. Our criterion for inclusion was simple: we looked for functional excellence. Of the dozens, sometimes of the hundreds of

items available of a particular type, we tried to find and include the finest examples. We confined ourselves to the things that would make for a graphically beautiful book as well as a visually beautiful home. But, while pedestrianism has been shunned, the sheer costliness of a given item has nothing to do with its appearance in these pages. If, by superior design, an item that is relatively inexpensive merits inclusion, chances are you will find it here. You will find, for instance, the Cadet toilet, one of the least expensive models on the market, but it also happens to have classically simple lines and purity of shape that costlier versions fail to surpass or even equal.

Some items have not been pictured because of their function. For example, a temperature-compensated shower valve that maintains a steady, pleasant temperature is hardly photogenic. Push-latches, those clever devices that eliminate the need for handles on cabinet doors, are not visual. A touch on the door panel and the spring pops the cabinet open. Another touch and the door is securely latched. In many of these cases, we have only been able to list the name of the manufacturer along with a description of the product.

Attention to Detail progresses through the house in a logical fashion. It begins with front doors. There are examples of doorways, entrance doors and exquisitely paneled doors. There are flush doors, solid doors, hollow-core doors, metal doors and closet doors. You will find door stains, knobs, hinges and numbers to give you a *sense* of and a feeling for the variety of items that is available.

The next topic: Floors. All kinds of spectacular, practical floors. Marble floors, granite floors, wooden

Detail of hand-carved door.

floors and parquet floors, styles of flooring and types of wood and wood stains for floors. Brilliant chunks of color. Dozens of new ideas to spark your imagination.

Then we move on to kitchens. The most expensive of all renovations, measured in cost per square foot, with bathrooms running a close second. The considerations here are practically endless. There are countertops, sinks, faucets, storage units and shelving. There is kitchen flooring: vinyl flooring and the new GenuWood flooring (a sliver of cork or wood is sandwiched between clear vinyl and a sheet of plastic and bonded together to look like the real thing but infinitely more durable). We even discovered a manufacturer who makes vinyl tiles in some ninety base colors. But, for as little as six square feet of tile, the company will perfectly match any color you supply whether it is a paint chip or fabric swatch or piece of wall paper. In addition, hanging storage units and a variety of kitchen cabinetry are also illustrated and discussed.

After kitchens, bathrooms are examined down to the last detail. We've devoted considerable space to bathroom tiles and bathroom colors. You will find color charts for matching the standard colors of the major manufacturers of bathroom fixtures — Kohler and American Standard — to the available colors of American Olean tiles, the leading line on the market. If, for example, you have an avocado toilet and a slate floor, here you will find the range of wall colors for achieving a pleasing effect overall. There are, in addition, bathtubs, shower enclosures, toilets, hot tubs and complete temperature-controlled environments, all manner of decorative basins and faucets, toilet paper holders, toothbrush holders and a good deal more.

Finally, there is a section on living rooms. It includes everything from moldings to wood paneling to switch plates to electronic intercoms. You will find interior knob sets for outside doors, and even a built-in outlet for hi-fi speakers.

Once you've taken a good hard look at the spectrum of alternatives available and narrowed the choices down to a couple that you really like, turn to the appendix at the back of the book where the manufacturers' names are listed and write for more detailed information. You will probably receive a general catalog of the manufacturer's line. This will do for a start. Go through it carefully, and decide exactly what items you want. For plumbing details, ask the manufacturer for "cuts" on those items. These are small, elaborately detailed brochures. In addition to illustrating and describing a particular item, they include the exact dimensions as well as any plumbing or electrical specifications your designer, architect or contractor might need to know.

Of all renovations, the simplest involve the basic replacement of objects. You take out a toilet and put a new one in. This simple task often necessitates other more complicated alterations, such as replacing the floor to better match the new toilet. The moment you decide to get more involved, you must have a budget and a carefully thought-out plan. And you may need professional help. But in every case, specific details are of paramount importance. To insure you get *exactly* what you want, you should know what the details are and *communicate* them thoroughly and clearly. The near-universal distrust of contractors arises less from incompetence and corner-cutting than from a basic failure to communicate, to spell everything out. It is not enough to tell a contractor: "Yes, put in a sink. And I want it done this way." You must have a floor plan. You must indicate the model and the style and the color of the sink you want. Of all the classic responses a contractor will give you when something turns out less than perfect, the most common (and the truest) is: "Oh, I didn't know you wanted it *that* way." When you hear those words, you are in for a good deal of disappointment, frustration, antipathy and, if you want the job done right, additional expense. To insure that you don't have these problems, be meticulously thorough the first time around.

To be able to communicate, there is a technical vocabulary to master, and you might not feel competent to deal with the contractor on a technical level. In that case, you might use an architect as a go-between, to make sure the full list of your specific needs is clearly understood by all concerned. An architect has studied shape, form, design, construction, materials and engineering so that he can design interior and exterior walls and make them stand, placing them in such a way that the spaces they create are pleasing, functional and satisfactory to the client. Designers, by way of contrast, do not have an architect's broad range of knowledge. And they tend to be specialists. There are, for example, bathroom designers or designers of kitchens. Designers are knowledgeable in a specific area and, unlike architects, they are not required to be licensed. The contractor deals in the final construction. He hires and works with a variety of craftsmen in executing the architect's design. A relatively new or, more accurately, rediscovered addition to this professional trio is the artisan, and they are enjoying increasing popularity. There are woodcarvers who gouge slabs of rare wood into doors that are delicately sculpted works of art. There are tilemakers who kiln bake whole

Air conditioner inserted into the window (top) and in the sleeve under the window (below).

sets of tiles according to color, sense of style, and design to fit directly into your room. In some cases, these artisans are taking the traditional place of designers because of the customized workmanship they contribute to the renovation project.

But regardless of the type of professional employed, all the successful homes we visited included the ongoing participation of the occupants as well. Without this involvement, by simply handing over the project to your designer or architect and saying: "Here, do this," you are not making the personal investment needed to truly enjoy the results later on.

There are, without a doubt, a fair number of people who might think these concerns supercilious. And it would be the height of pretention to say that they are wrong, that they are aesthetically limited, but their outlook is somehow deficient. One of my good friends owns a thirty-eight-foot yacht. He has no car. He walks to work. He lives in a modest home. He is preoccupied with that boat. Wonderful! I would be the last one to insist that this person spend as much time on his home as he does on his yacht, or even concern himself at all, if his primary interest lies elsewhere. Some people own heavy-duty racing cars and aren't concerned with their homes. Fine. It is a fascinating activity and good luck to him. Paying attention to the details of one's home is involvement in another kind of activity, but one with which an extraordinary number of people concern themselves. Why? Certainly because of the expense involved. Because of the tremendous personal investment of time and thought. By their concern and participation they are protecting that investment. For when the renovation is finished, everywhere you look, all the little details that you see, collectively become your home.

The detailing of a house is a soft understatement of visual delights. You walk into a room and think: "I really did a good job. The molding on the wall, the door knobs and hinges, the lighting switchplates, the balusters of the stairs — everything works. Everything is just right." Whenever you walk into that room it strikes you, either on a conscious or a subliminal level. You feel a certain undercurrent of pleasure. And you think: "How nice it is to be here." To achieve that purity of sensation, it is worth the patience, the extra time, the occasional aggravation, that go part and parcel with a concern for detail. Whether an air conditioner is inserted into a sleeve *under* the window or you actually put it *into* the window — those are the choices. One gives you a clean line and easy maintenance; the other does not.

In traveling across the country taking photographs for my previous books (MADE WITH OAK, LIVING PLACES, GOOD LIVES and ROOMS WITH A VIEW), and in being interviewed on television talk shows and radio programs, I am invariably asked: Who are these books for? Who buys them? Who reads them? By way of an answer, I tell how I can go to a place like Woodstock, visit a homespun, folksy house full of antiques and hand-made things, and there, on the living room shelves, will be my books. The owners are concerned about where they live. They buy the books to see what other people have done, to draw some inspiration from the stunning rooms. Then I travel to Beverly Hills and visit the most carefully designed and decorated of houses. And I find my books on the shelves as well. Those homeowners, too, are concerned. So I can only conclude that this sense of concern is rather widespread, spanning all age brackets and socio-economic

levels. As the burgeoning urban renewal movement indicates, an increasing number of the nation's homeowners are turning their attention to detail. And whether they live in the homespun atmosphere of a Woodstock or the golden glitter of a Beverly Hills — it shows.

Herbert Wise

New York
September, 1979

Front Doors

First impressions are important. The front door is the first part of your house most people encounter. Doors can be paneled, recessed or raised. A wooden door can be painted any color or stained to show off the wood.

Mail Slots

Sleeker than a mail box and more secure — the mail slides
inside, safe from the street — a mail slot should match the style
of your door. Polished brass is traditional, brushed chrome more
contemporary. In addition to the question of finish, there is the
question of scale. A large or wide door takes a longer mail slot.
Its placement, vertical or horizontal, is up to you.

Door Numbers

Door numbers can be decorative as well as useful, as plain and subdued or bold and obvious as you want. Numbers come in brass and wood and plastic, in gleaming enamel and inexpensive foam. Many can be painted to match exterior woodwork or to contrast with the color of your door. (The line of nine numerals in the middle of this page shows the versatility of painted foam.) As you choose numbers for your front door, be aware not just of color and finish but also of the styles of the numbers themselves.

Numbers as well as letters come in a wide variety of typefaces, some with a clean and modern look, others with the curves and curlicues of an earlier age. The Victorian gilded numbers offer an especially elegant alternative. (page 18, 1)

Door Knockers

We are accustomed to seeing bold brass knockers on traditional homes. Original knockers can be found at auctions and in antique stores. Contemporary copies are available from many manufacturers. The brass can be pure and gleaming or antiqued to a more subtle burnished glow. Wrought iron knockers to silhouette against a painted wooden door is another alternative for traditional or Spanish-style houses, particularly those with wrought-iron gates. To accentuate a modern door, consider a stark sliver of chrome (13) or a heavier design (10) in the same material.

6

7

8

9

10

11

12

13

14

Door Designs

Behind all the accessories is the door itself, and the choices are enormous. You know you want a paneled wooden door, but what kind? Study some options, left. The standard steel door comes pre-painted in the colors below.

Interior Doors

Exterior doors are just the beginning. Interior doors can be solid or hollow, fitted with panes of leaded or etched glass, paneled or louvered. You'll need doors for rooms, for closets, showers, passageways. Doors should be consistent with the style of the house. You may want different kinds of doors in different areas, but it's best to keep to a pattern — the same style of door for all the bedrooms, for example. Doors can be painted to match the room or to contrast with it, picking up a color from the fabric or furnishings. If you prefer natural wood, you may want to have wooden doors stained to match the shade of the floors.

Don't be afraid to replace interior doors if the existing ones don't meet your needs. Interesting doors are an easy way to make an ordinary room distinctive, and they are a lot less expensive than major architectural renovations.

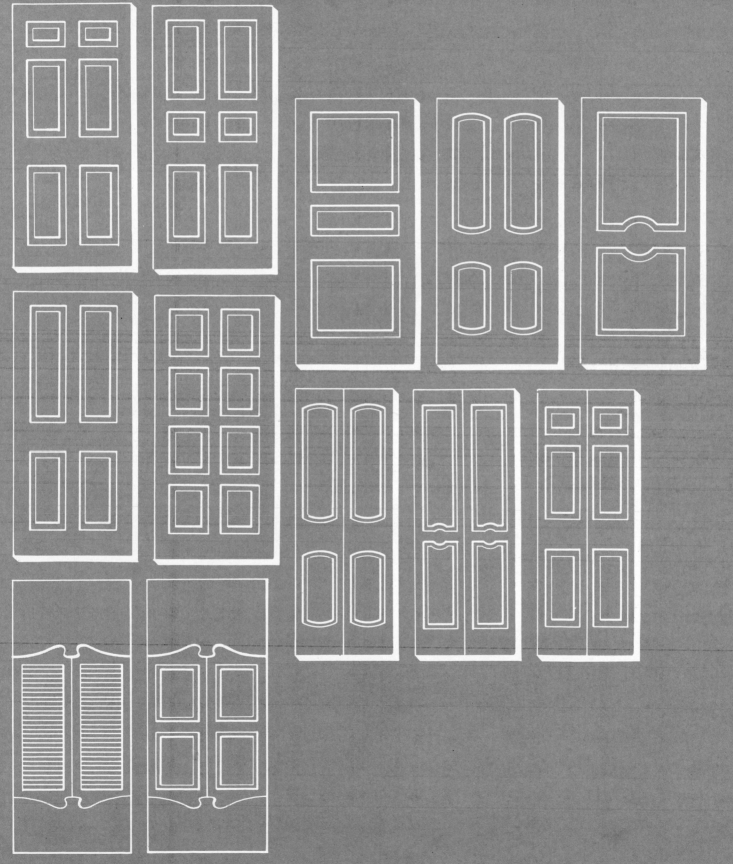

Hinges

Once you've chosen a door, turn your attention to its hinges. Hinges can be recessed and hidden (10) or made more obvious and in keeping with the style of the door. There are ornate strap hinges (1), hinges with removable pins for ease of installation (7), butt hinges (6) and H hinges (11). If you're lucky, you may find an old house with the original brass hinges still in place. If so, don't paint them over. Clean and polish to show them at their best. If not, antiques or good copies are easy to come by. For a contemporary house, you'll also want the appropriate hardware.

Hooks

For maximum storage in minimum space, nothing is quicker and simpler than a hook. Hooks can stand in for closets and cabinets, provide a convenient resting place for visitors' coats, suspend a tool or towel just where you need it, and be decorative as well as utilitarian.

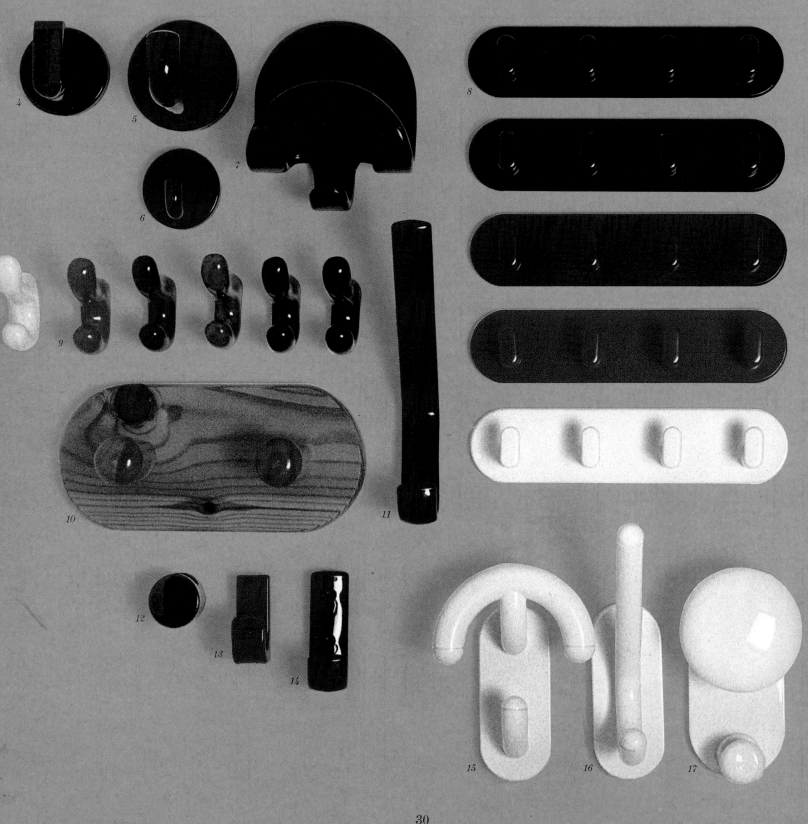

A strip of bright plastic hooks will provide color down a dark passageway; giant white ones have an almost sculptural impact. Some recessed hooks are virtually invisible until you need them. Again, there are hooks for all styles and periods. The four-pronged antique coat hook below is traditional English brass. The slim black one is neoprene-coated steel. When looking for a spot to hang a hook, don't forget the ceiling. Lack of wall space needn't keep you from getting hooked.

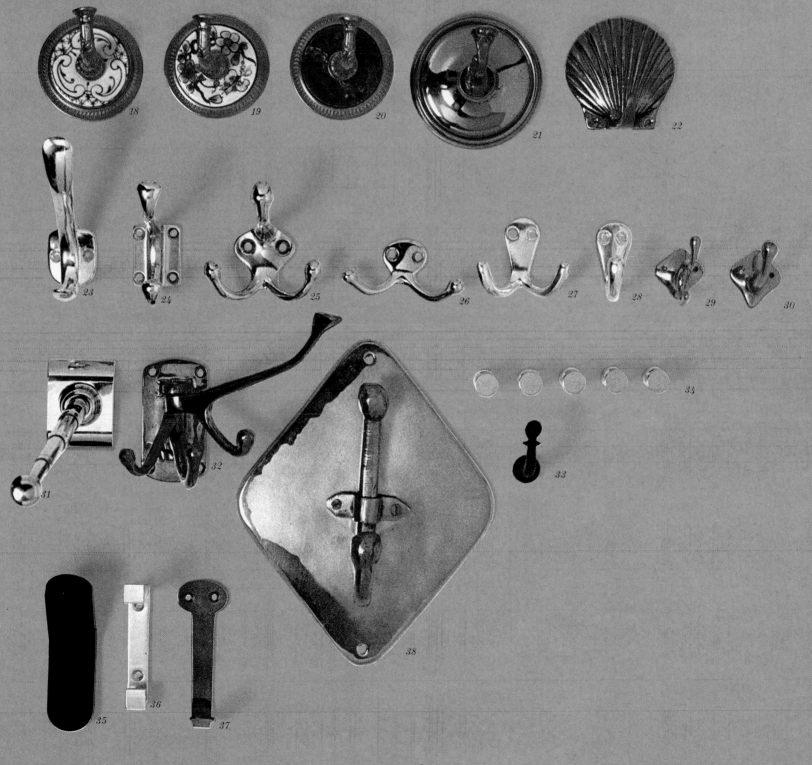

Marble

Marble can be elegant as well as durable, as this classic entrance hall demonstrates. The samples below will give you an idea of the wide range of colors and textures that this oldest of flooring materials affords. The Building Stone Institute, which supplied these samples, can give you the name of the supplier nearest to you. Like all natural materials, marble develops a beautiful patina as it ages. Its upkeep is minimal.

Earth Tiles

Man-made and therefore more regular than stone or wood flooring, quarry tile gets its richly colored warmth from natural red clay. True quarry tile, the kind shown below, comes in simple squares, hexagons and the other shapes shown here (3). It is unglazed and consequently not suitable for bathrooms, though it works beautifully for most other rooms in the house. If you do want to expose quarry tiles to moisture, you can seal them with wax.

A better alternative for bathrooms, however, is Primitive tiles from American Olean (2). These are slightly glazed and come in a broader spectrum of colors than quarry tiles, though they retain the same sense of earth and sun. Fully glazed tiles from Mexico, also illustrated below (4), are fired just like pottery. Both Primitive and Mexican tiles are available in several shapes as is quarry tile.

Slate and Granite

These and the hundreds of other varieties of stone can be finished to your specifications. Polished, brushed, sanded and thermal finishes change the color and texture. In most yards, a wide selection of sizes is readily available. Stonemasons will be glad to custom quarry in unusual lengths and thicknesses.

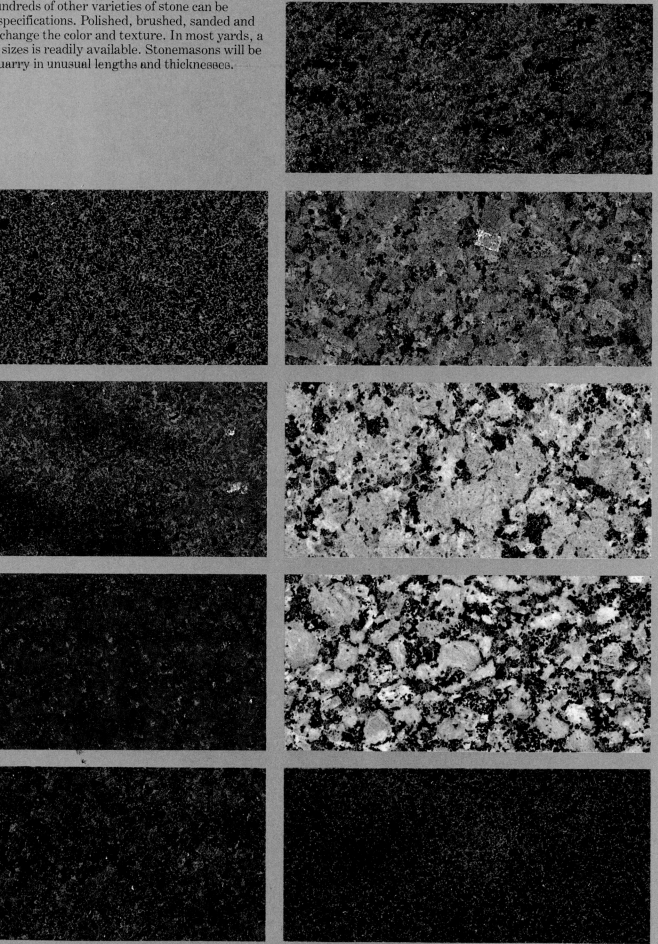

Wood

Wood floors can be composed of simple, straight-laid boards (either wide or narrow) or patterned in more elaborate designs with names like herringbone or Versailles. They can be stained dark or pale, or made of several different shades of wood. But even the plainest wood floors require care. Regular waxing is one way to do it. Easier maintenance can be obtained if the floor is sealed with polyurethane after being sanded and stained. You can refinish a floor yourself or hire someone to do it for you. Professionals use enormous, very stable sanding machines which cover large areas at one time. As many as five grits of sandpaper may be required to insure an even satin finish.

GenuWood

In some part of the house — in front of the kitchen counter, for example — constant walking may make wood floors impractical. There are many substitutes, but if wood is what you want, you might consider GenuWood. A thin sliver of real wood or cork encased in clear vinyl, each piece of GenuWood is slightly different from the others because it has natural materials as a base. As these samples demonstrate, GenuWood comes in a wide range of colors. Maintenance couldn't be simpler.

It never fails. When the party gets good, everyone ends up in the kitchen. The kitchen is the warmest room in the house — in atmosphere, if not temperature — and the one in which we spend the largest portion of our waking hours. It is also the most expensive room to build or remodel.

Kitchens

Whether your taste runs to homey country kitchens or gleaming expanses of Corian and chrome, your options are almost endless. The most important consideration is what and how you like to cook.

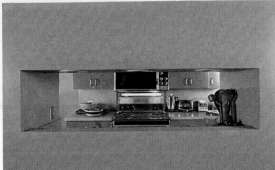

2

3

Kitchen Conversion

When the new owner converted the library of an elegant New York townhouse into a kitchen, he wanted to retain its original atmosphere. He also wanted the room to function as an informal dining room without making guests feel that they were eating in the kitchen. Wood cabinets were built to hide utensils and utilities, and to blend handsomely with the classic oak herringbone floor. The double-paneled door near the sink opens out to screen the clean-up area (wastebasket, dishwasher, sink) from diners. Instead of a "big white box" — his description of most refrigerators — there are two under-the-counter units, one a freezer, the other a fridge. The countertop is red Vermont granite, impervious to heat, staining or chipping. The cabinet that shields the sink holds crockery and glassware as well as work space for a toaster, built-in blender, food processor and magnetic knife rack. In lieu of ceiling fixtures, powerful recessed lights illuminate the work areas, while track lighting (see page 86) creates highlights.

Kitchen Planning

There is no standard plan for the perfect kitchen. What you need depends on how you use the room: exclusively for cooking, for cooking and dining, to accommodate a small family or a large one. Graph paper can help make your needs concrete within the space available. Use a half-inch scale (i.e., a half-inch equals one foot). Some early sketches of kitchens are shown here to demonstrate how simple and practical planning can be. Study traffic patterns when you arrange appliances. It is convenient to have all the clean-up equipment in one place, and to create food preparation areas close to the stove to minimize walking and

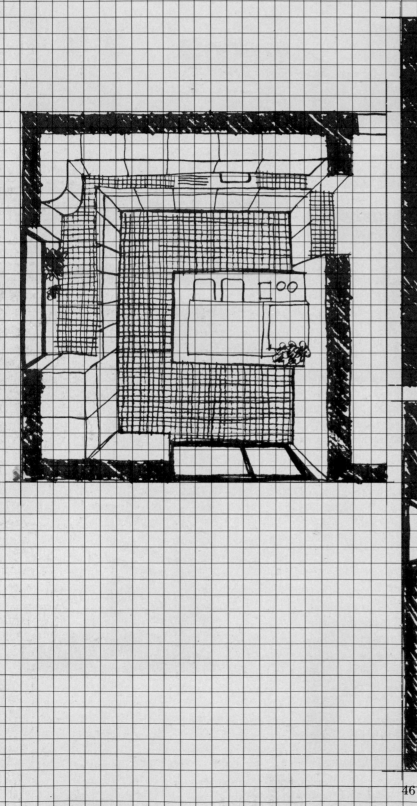

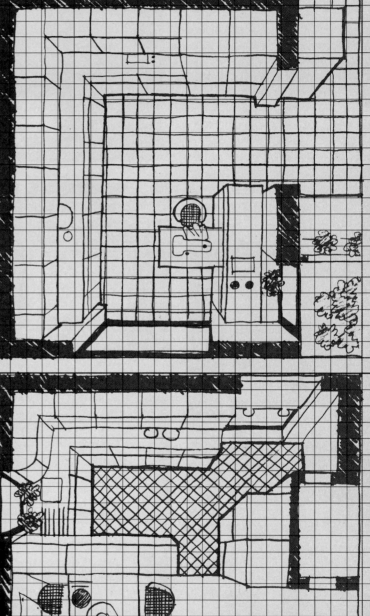

spills. A U-shaped counter that permits food preparation on one
side of the U and cooking and serving on the other works well
for many people. Your drawing need not be technically
sufficient for the contractor, but will help an architect
or designer translate your requirements into final plans.

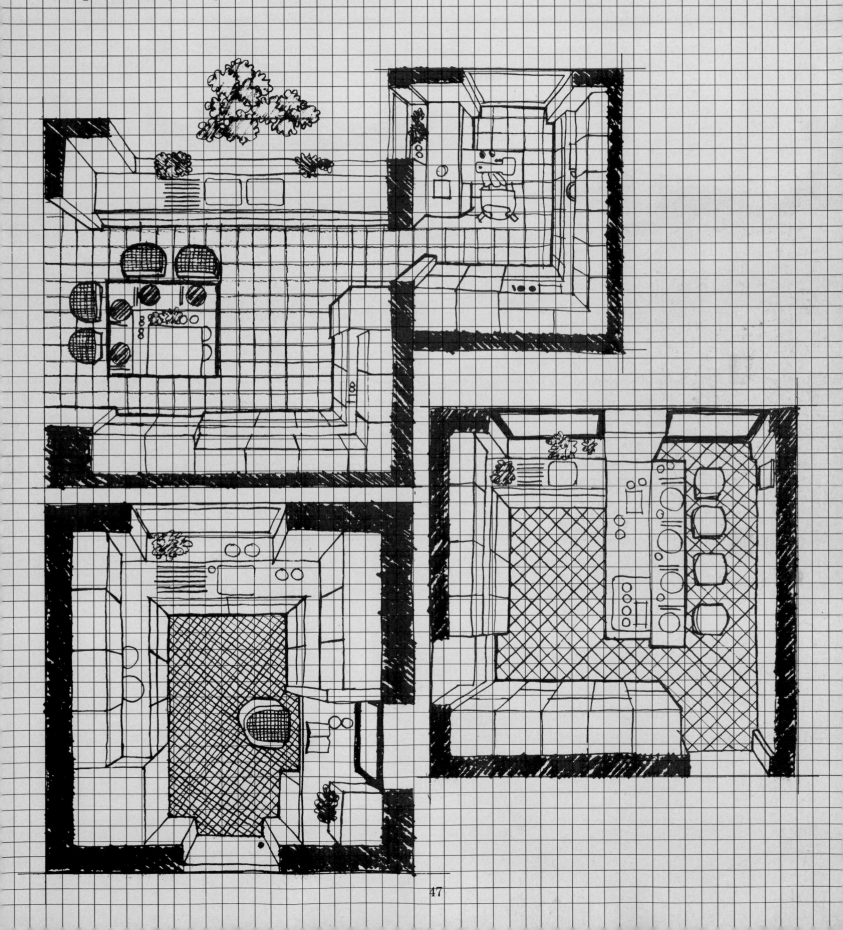

Cooktops

We couldn't show you every kind of cooktop or even list every manufacturer, but here is a list of the major choices you have to make:

Gas versus electric (or both on one range)
Smooth-top heating surface versus burners
Grill or no grill
Controls up front or at the side
Space-saver size or professional multi-burner capacity.

1

2

Alpes-Inox

For variety (see page 55) and high style, the interchangeable components made by Italy's Alpes-Inox are in a class by themselves. Cooks traditionally prefer the immediacy afforded by gas burners, but electric burners offer steadiness of heat and precise thermal control. These satin-finish, heavy-gauge stainless steel cooktops come with gas burners, electric burners or a combination in the same unit. The gas stovetops are all pilotless, with an automatic electric ignition and a thermal-electric safety device that turns off the burner if the flame blows out by accident.

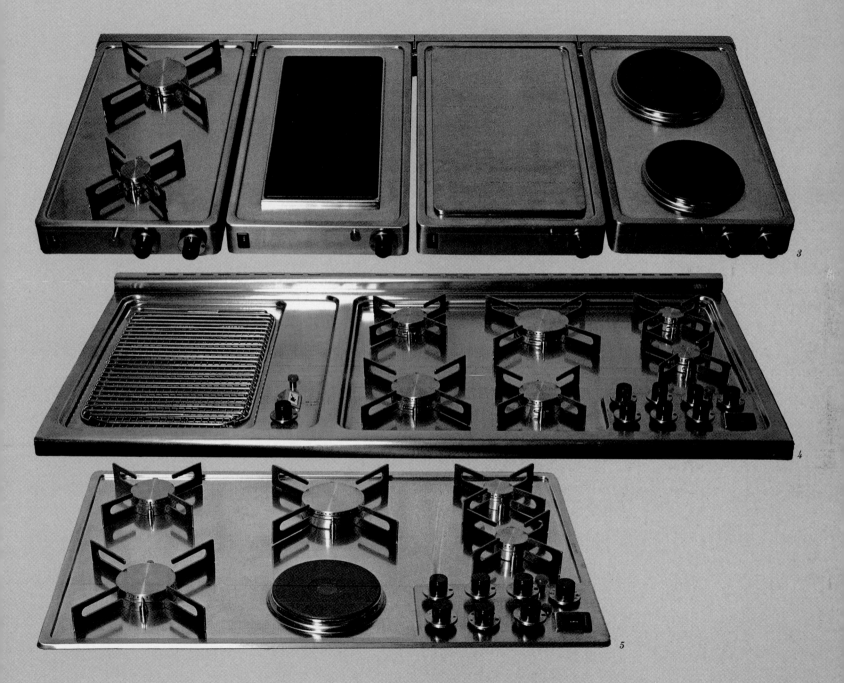

3

4

5

Indoor Grills

A fascinating array of flexible grills and rotisserie units is available from Jenn-Air. Components are interchangeable for maximum flexibility. Units include built-in, range-level exhaust fans (no hood to collect grease) that vent through the wall. Conventional cooking surfaces come in a choice of smooth-top or electric burner.

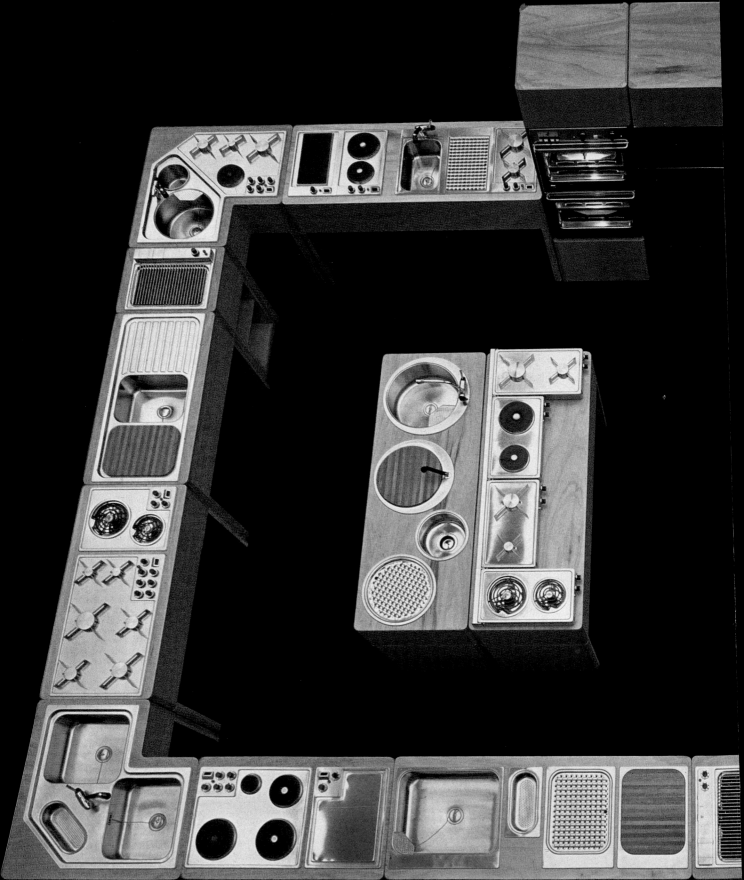

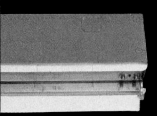

An Array of Tools

This is the range of kitchen appliances available from just one manufacturer (Alpes-Inox). Imagine how many more are on the market. That is why it is worth doing research before making your choices: to be aware of all your options when you are just starting to plan. Remember that you don't have to do a whole kitchen at once. Appliances can be replaced one by one. It is a good idea to find a manufacturer you like so that as you make the changes, each new piece will match the others in color and style. If you have a small or irregular kitchen, look for scaled-down appliances designed to stack or fit into corners.

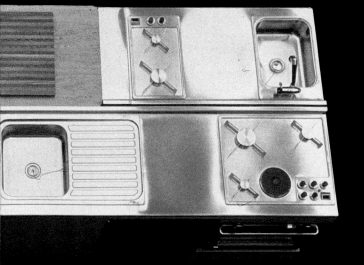

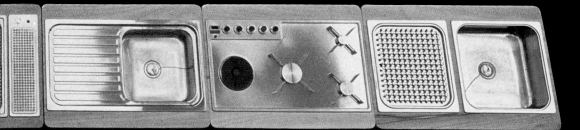

The Kitchen Sink: Enamel

Colorful and easy to clean, enamel has always been a popular material for sinks. Enamel sinks come with single or double or triple compartments in a wide variety of shapes and sizes. Some include optional cutting boards, drain baskets or disposal units. The primary consideration in choosing the size of a sink is the size of your countertop.

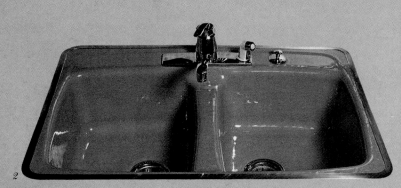

2

1

3

4

5

Dishwashing and food preparation needs are also important factors in your decision. A double sink provides one sink for washing, another for rinsing, for example. The major disadvantage of enamel: it can chip if heavy pots are dropped on it. Properly cared for, however, it should last for years.

6

7

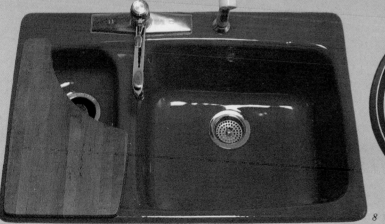

8

9

The Kitchen Sink: Stainless Steel

Stainless steel comes in only one color but an almost infinite number of styles. You rarely have to worry about size when choosing a sink, since models are readily available from many manufacturers in two-inch increments. There are single, double and triple-bowl sinks. Most are self-rimming. A shallow bowl is convenient for food preparation; a drainboard will protect your countertop from excess water. (Too much moisture is bad for butcher block.)

Corian

Although not a natural material, Corian® by DuPont has many advantages. It is solid straight through, making it hard to damage and easy to repair. Scratches and knife marks can be sandpapered away. Corian is impervious to water. Its non-porous surface is almost impossible to stain and wipes clean with a damp cloth. Corian will stand higher than ordinary temperatures, but a protective pad should be used for extremely hot pots. Its unique beauty lies in the uniformity of a Corian sink-and-countertop combination which produces a long, sleek line perfect for the contemporary kitchen. Corian is available in colors as well as pure white and can be custom-cut

1

2

3

to any dimension. Because it is a solid synthetic, there are no texture or grain problems to take into consideration when cutting Corian.

Below are General Electric's standard appliance colors. Those to the right are the colors of handles and knobs from The Ironmonger.

Kitchen Faucets

Some people prefer the sleekness of the single lever, others the subtle temperature variations possible with double faucets. Sinks come with holes to accommodate the faucet(s), spigot and other kinds of hardware such as soap dispensers, spray hoses, boiling-water spouts for making tea and coffee. The faucet(s) and spigot can be set directly into the holes of the sink. They are also available attached to a shiny metal "deck" that can be installed to cover the holes of the sink. The decision is yours, but be sure to coordinate sink and faucets. Other options are high, curved spouts (11) for ease of dishwashing, and hospital

11

handles (17) that can be turned on with the elbows if your hands are full. Chicago also makes valves that operate with foot pedals (not shown).

17

12

13

14

15

16

Kitchens Big and Small

The Vulcan restaurant gas range below is the chef's delight, but some of us have to make do with a small apartment-size unit. One-piece kitchens come in a variety of narrow widths with either electric or gas burners. Each also contains a refrigerator, freezer, oven, sink and overhead storage cabinets. Another alternative for the L-shaped kitchen is the efficient sink-and-cooktop combination at right. Who says everyone needs miles of counter space?

4

Countertops

There is more than one way to build a countertop. Don't make snap judgments about what materials you can afford. Stone tops often equal the plastics in price, and, since they have been on (or in) the earth for millions of years, have an unequaled durability record. Granite, slate and marble resist water and wear with ease, though marble will stain and slate will flake if put under great pressure. But well-worn doesn't mean shoddy — one trusts a butcher who has worn his chopping block down after years of toil. Butcher block looks wonderful and eliminates all need for cutting boards if you don't drain dishes on it. Don't cut on Corian or Formica. They don't benefit from knife marks.

Formica

This colorful chart shows fewer than half the colors available for this practical and ubiquitous building material. Formica can be cut in any shape and used to cover walls, counters, cabinets and drawers for a completely coordinated kitchen. Because Formica® wipes clean so easily, it makes kitchen maintenance a snap. For Formica to wear well, it is important that it be properly prepared — the plastic must be glued down under pressure. Otherwise, the edges tend to peel, chip and crack and a new room will look shoddy quickly, with none of the well-worn grace of other, more natural products.

Kitchen Tile

Flooring is only one of the ways to use tile in the kitchen. Quarry tile (below) makes a versatile and warm-toned covering for a countertop. Ceramic tile is equally useful as a back-splash behind the stove. Easy to clean, tile is a great solution to the greasy-wall problem. Either kind of tile can also be used on the floor, but ceramic tile will crack if you drop anything heavy. When buying tiles, it is always a good idea to get a few extras to replace any damaged squares in the years ahead.

1

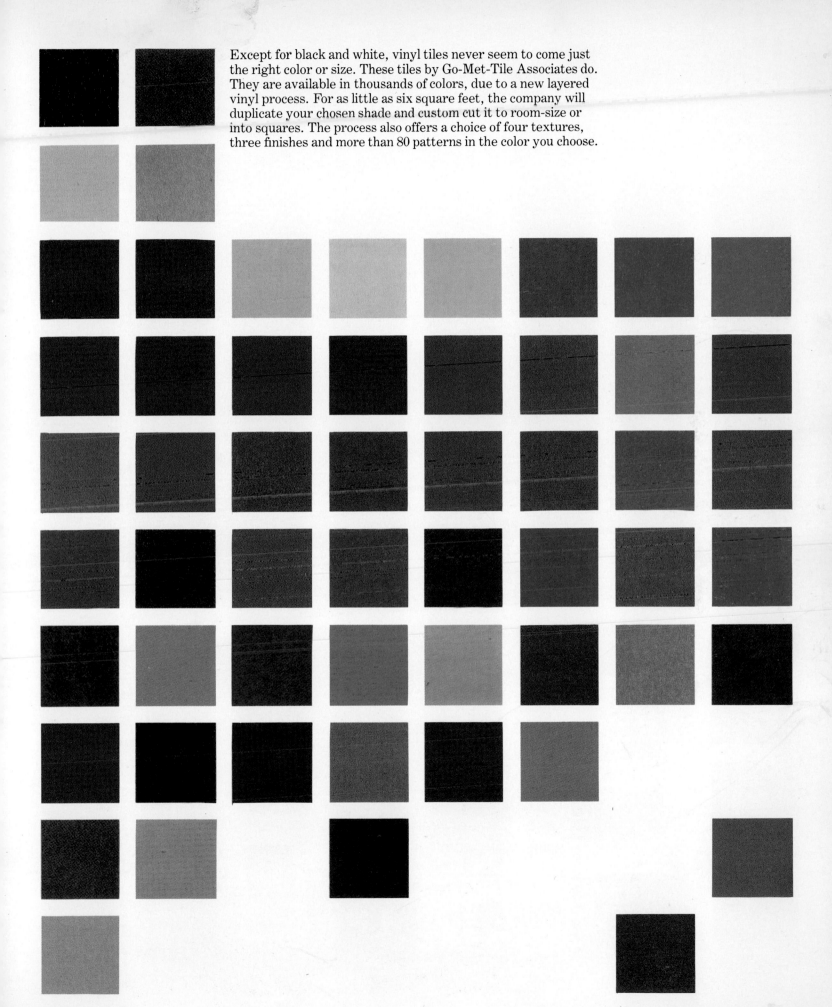

Except for black and white, vinyl tiles never seem to come just the right color or size. These tiles by Go-Met-Tile Associates do. They are available in thousands of colors, due to a new layered vinyl process. For as little as six square feet, the company will duplicate your chosen shade and custom cut it to room-size or into squares. The process also offers a choice of four textures, three finishes and more than 80 patterns in the color you choose.

The kitchen is a workroom, much like a laboratory or an office. Success often depends on organization, and the best chefs know that their efficiency demands order and cleanliness. All of which require cabinets and drawers. Though you can use these pieces of furniture to hide clutter, the best kitchen cabinets are in fact

1

2

carefully organized. The assemblage of drawers and cabinets below is a model of the art — almost too perfect to be real (though of course it is). Neat rows of groceries fill the shelves at left. Dishes are stacked or arranged on racks, center. Under one cabinet, utensils hang on hooks, handy to the stove and food-preparation counter. Basket drawers of varying depths provide additional storage at right, as do small racks on the broom-closet door. The smaller photographs at lower right demonstrate other solutions to the problem. The built-in cutting board is an excellent way to acquire a few extra feet of counter space.

3

5

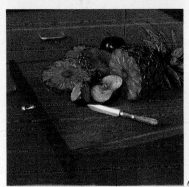

6

4

Extra Storage

When you have a lot to store and little room to store it, search for space wherever you can find it.

St. Charles offers special drawer cabinets to stash cutting boards, pots and pans, and wine under the counter. The trash bin usually goes under the sink because no one wants to look at it and it is convenient for scraping plates.

When you have filled up your counters, take to the walls and hang pots, coats and even a small shelf for the kitchen clock.

Versatile Shelving

One of the most durable and attractive materials for shelving is vinyl-clad steel. The shelves can be installed in closets for food or clothing, and come in depths of 9 to 20 inches and lengths of up to 12 feet. They are fitted to the wall with brackets or screws. Their open construction allows air to circulate through the closet, which prevents mildew and infestations. Another shelving alternative is the modular wall unit. The version below offers clothes rods, shelves and drawers in combinations that can be assembled to fit almost any space. The same manufacturer makes a cabinet with a fold-away table and another with a revolving bookcase that conceals a bed.

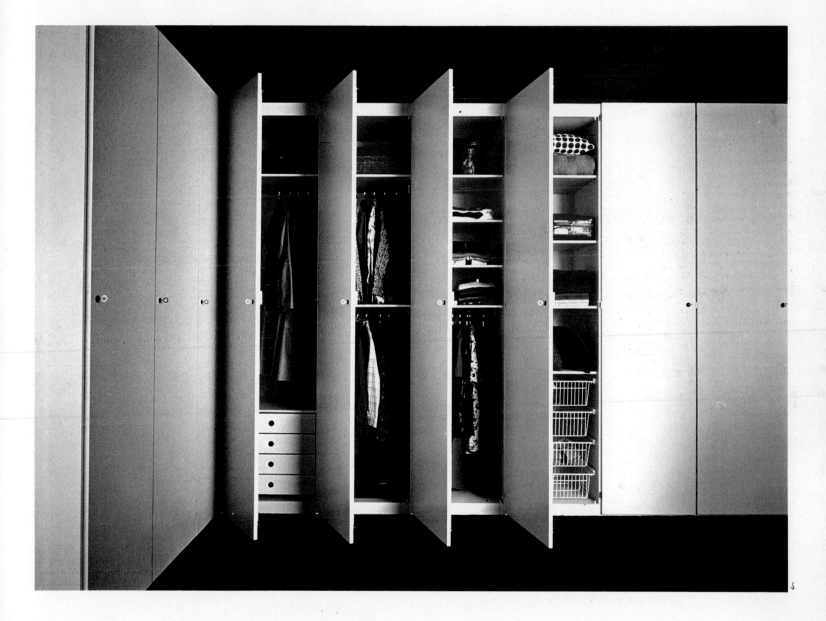

4

Handles

A handle is a simple item — it is the choice that is difficult. What are the considerations? The style of the cabinet and the room will dictate the color and design of the handle. Scale is important in determining the size of the handle. Practicality is another consideration. You probably wouldn't want recessed or rubberized handles for the kitchen, but they might work well in a child's room. In the cooking area, plastic or simple aluminum

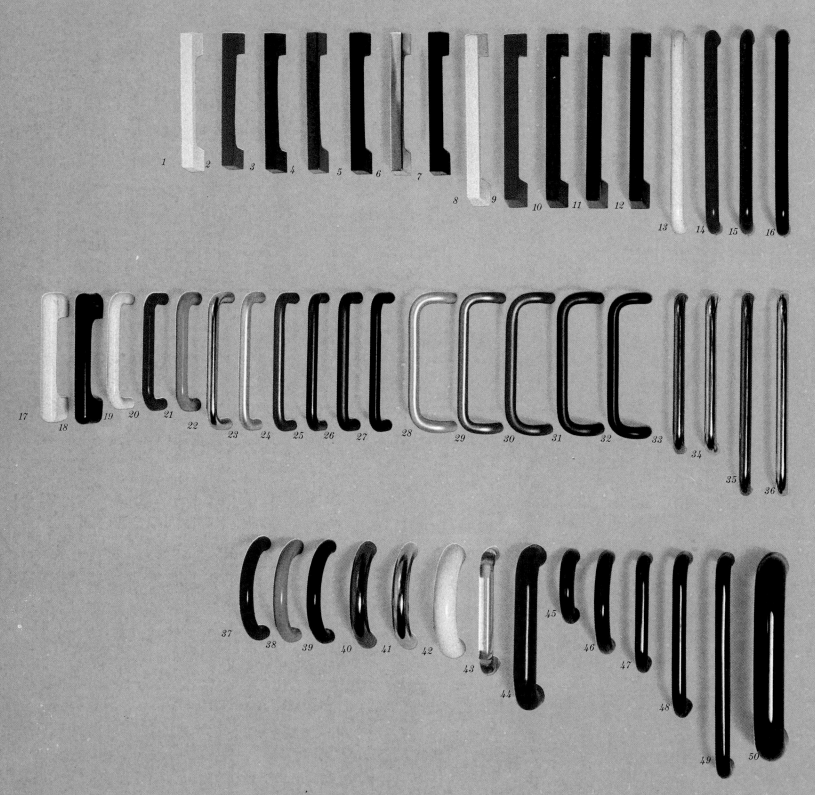

handles are favorites because they fit with almost any style and are easy to clean and to grasp with messy hands. Because there are so many alternatives, you may also want to choose according to the way the handle feels when you hold it. Some have a solid heft that makes them a pleasure to use. If you have large hands, you may find very small, recessed handles difficult to maneuver. We can't show the push latch, a device fixed inside the cabinet that makes the door open with a touch and push closed with another. A push latch requires no handle at all.

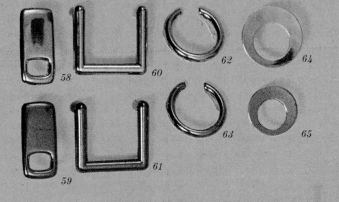

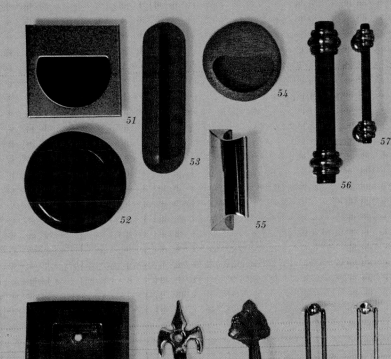

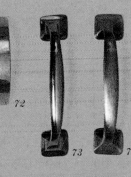

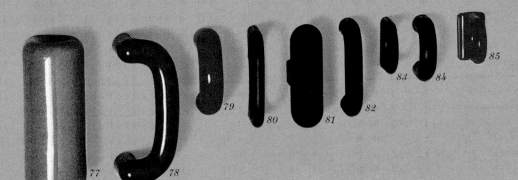

Knobs

Choosing knobs is very similar to choosing handles. Because knobs have no interior edges to trap food, they are especially good for kitchens. Patterned porcelain knobs make particularly pretty accessories for bedrooms.

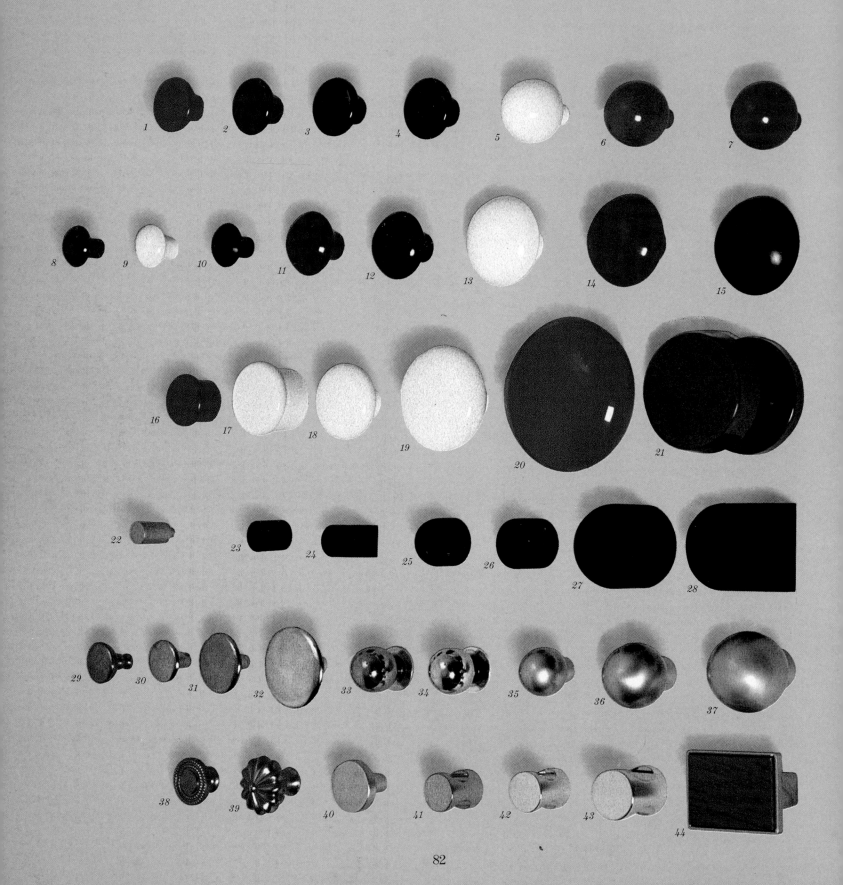

Because knobs and handles are relatively inexpensive, you may find them especially useful in adding distinction to pieces of furniture that are otherwise uninteresting. Replacing the knobs on a plain, unpainted chest of drawers is far more economical than replacing the chest and it may enable you to accomplish the same objective. Most good hardware stores offer a wide variety of handles and knobs.

There is no single more important factor in stressing
the shape and quality of a room than lighting. If a room is flatly
lit, even the most beautifully designed spaces appear
uninteresting because the lighting does not direct the eye to
the salient features. Lamps, under-counter lights and other
accent lights help, but one excellent solution is track lighting.
The versatility of placing a spotlight anywhere on an
electrified track allows the renovator who is unsure of the final
placement of furniture or art the flexibility he or she requires.
Many tracks now feature two individual circuits per track so
that one does not have to use all the lights at the same time.

Track Lighting

When selecting track lighting, be sure the fixtures are compatible with the tracks—it is wisest to buy both from the same manufacturer. Fixtures can be fitted with several kinds of bulbs. These are listed in the chart on page 146, along with the light patterns and candlepower each offers.

Track for lighting can be installed in several different ways. They can be recessed (8) so that the track is flush against the ceiling or surface mounted on the ceiling (9), which is a good solution for renovators because it does not require

1

2

3

4

replastering around the tracks, or even suspended with cables or stanchions (3). Track lighting can be an important feature in the design of a room. Below, a highly architectural chrome track becomes an exciting light sculpture. Alternatively, it can recede into the background. Some designers prefer to place white lights on white ceilings and focus attention on the objects that are lit. Though track lighting is clearly contemporary, it can work in more traditional settings if it is concealed. Partially hiding the lights between the beams of a ceiling is one good solution.

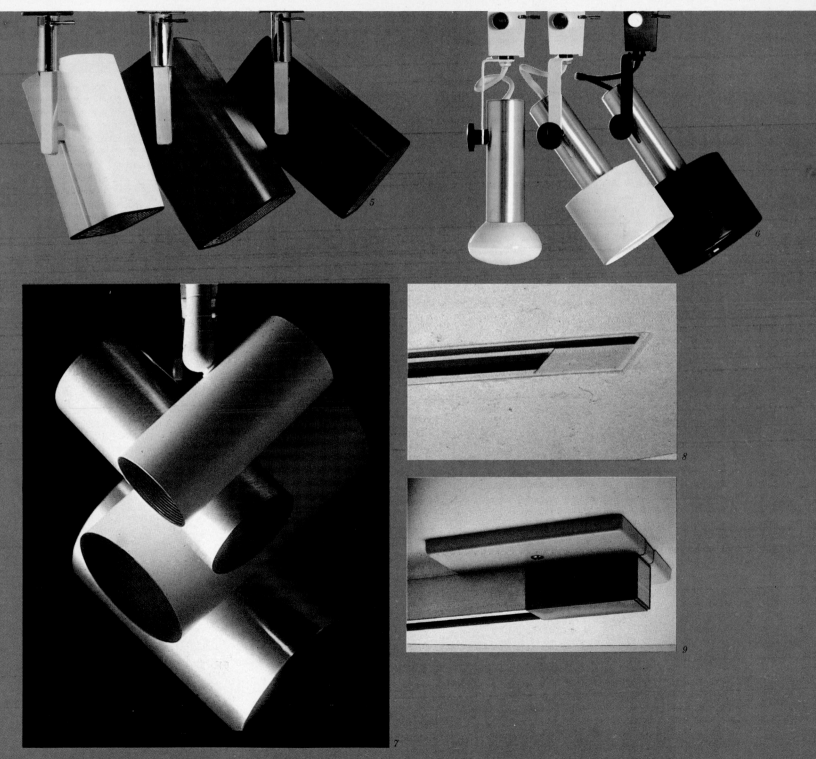

Task Lighting

Task lighting conserves energy by bringing good light to the
work area instead of to the whole room. A new fluorescent
task light by Lightolier (2) eliminates glare with a special lens
that bounces reflected light away from the work surface.
Fluorescent lights set in brightly colored boxes (3) or natural
oak fixtures (1) look anything but institutional.

Among the special features of track lighting are wall washers, (page 87, 5) fixtures that incorporate mirrors to bathe the walls with light, enhancing unusual paneling or other fine materials. Track lights were first widely used in art galleries and are still one of the best ways to focus attention on your artworks.

4

Walls

Paneling relieves you of the obligation to repaint every several years. What an advantage that is. But before you paint or panel, you must complete all the electrical work. Think about hiding the wires for stereo speakers, telephone and intercom inside the walls. In most cities, the phone company will prewire your house if you give them sufficient notice. Your electrician can install a high-quality intercom. Talk-A-Phone is the best around for ease of operation and clarity of tone. He can also take care of your stereo-speakers. Anyone can learn to replace light-switch covers. If you do not like the standard ones, most electrical supply houses will order handsome brass or steel non-beveled oversize plates to your specifications. Good hardware stores also have an endless supply of designs for every sort of room.

1

3

Brick

An indoor and outdoor building material, brick has an elegance all its own. There are many sorts of new brick. One kind, by Alwine, simulates the mellow rosiness of the weathered buildings of colonial Virginia. Smooth brick, samples of which are pictured below, can look completely contemporary. Brick has the advantage of being fireproof. Many home and apartment dwellers are removing the plaster from their walls to reveal the rough old brick underneath. Newly exposed brick tends to get powdery. A coat of silicone can be applied to hold back the dust. Some people prefer to paint the brick walls to take advantage of its texture. Old brick can be porous and might require numerous coats of paint.

2

Moldings

If you enjoy visiting old houses, you have probably been amazed by their rich and ornamental plaster cast moldings. New buildings no longer come with such moldings but you can simulate that effect with these embossed hardwood moldings by Driwood. The company offers a wide range of sizes and shapes that can be painted to look like plaster, or stained if you prefer the warmth of wood. The moldings are equally suited for baseboards, window and door casings, chair rails and wainscotting trim.

Balusters and Newel Posts

Some terminology first. Stairs come in sections, each with its own name. There is the tread (the part you step on), the riser (the upright portion between treads), the handrail (the banister), the baluster (the individual posts between the treads and the handrail) and the newel post (the larger posts at the head, foot and sometimes middle of a staircase). All of

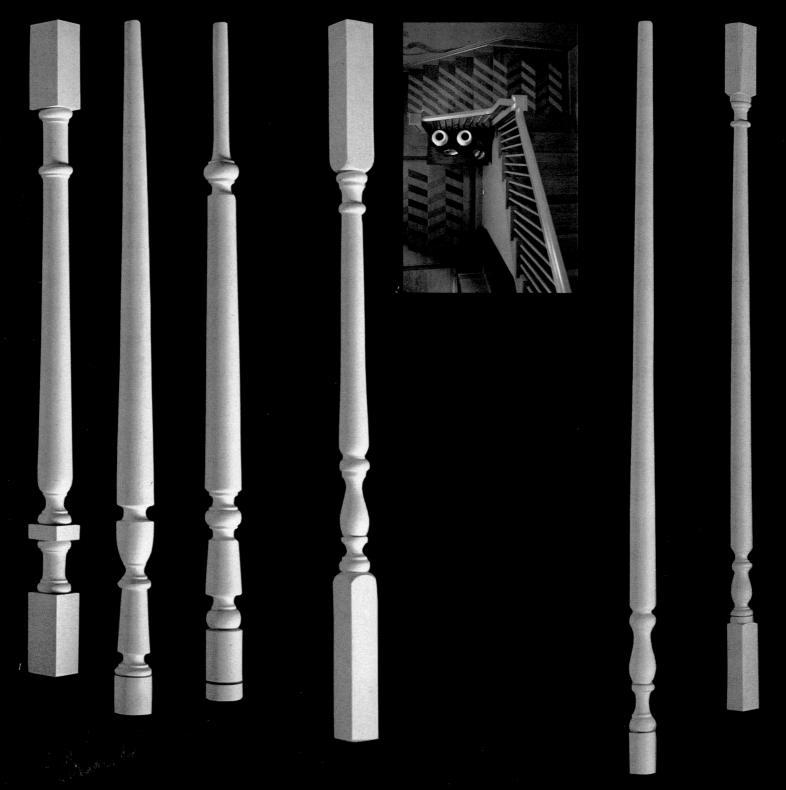

of your house. Risers and treads can be stained, painted or carpeted. They can be completely carpeted or only partially carpeted with runners that let the treads show at either side. (In the latter case, you may want to secure the runners with decorative metal carpet rods at the back of each tread.) Handrails, balusters and newel posts come in a number of designs. If you have a traditional house, research the shapes that were characteristic of the style of the house or furnishings. The wood balusters illustrated here, both stock and custom-made, are from American Wood Column.

Spiral Stairs

Architects favor spiral stairs for their complex forms and intricate structures. Custom designs are very expensive, especially if the handrails are handmade. On this page, are some alternatives: free-form plaster (1), which eliminates the need for a handrail; a straight-rail staircase with landings instead of curves (6). Another possibility is a pre-fabricated wooden spiral staircase. Those made by York (2, 4, 7) come in two sizes and three finishes. They function as a primary stairway. For a space-saving second stair, you may want to look at the metal spiral-stair kits from Mylen (3, 5).

4

7

6

5

1

2

3

4

The Master Bath

After the kitchen, the bathroom is the most costly to improve. Nevertheless, it is a frequent target of remodelers. Natural materials—marble, granite, slate—are well suited to a room where steam and water abound, as are tile and mirror. In addition to the usual complement of sinks and tubs, other features can be built in. One of these is a separate stall shower which offers the additional luxury of conversion to a sauna or steam room. The Thermosol steam generator can create a steam room with a mechanism no larger than a breadbox. Connected to water and electricity, the installation is invisible. Bathrooms may also include a raised platform for the tub, double sink (a boon for couples or families with children) and heated towel racks, though in these energy-scarce days, they may be an unnecessary luxury.

1

2

3

An Interesting Bathroom

Marble and wood combine here for a bathroom of unusual architectural integrity. The walls and countertop are a warm marble that picks up the golden tone of the wooden vanity, towel bar and shower-unit frame. The vanity is louvered to accentuate the line of the marble. The sink is set below the counter, its faucets mounted in it, breaking the surface symmetry as little as possible. Similarly, the tub faucets are attached directly to the vanity. Wall washers in the recessed lighting along the wall bathe it with light, subtly bringing out the texture of the stone. Further lighting is strategically placed for shaving and showering. The shower unit, reflected in the mirror, contains a Thermosol, permitting it to do double duty as a steam room.

Shower Enclosures

Where space and cost are considerations, the one-piece molded shower enclosure may be the answer. Pre-formed, yet available in a range of shapes and sizes, these practical units leave the worry of water leakage and expensive tiling behind. If you want a more elaborate combination with a choice of dry or wet heat, sun (sunlamp, anyway) or rain, the Environment (4) by Kohler will provide it all. Choosing a showerhead is both a question of styling and of versatility. The better all-brass models allow adjustment of the spray to a broad range of volumes and strengths from fine to heavy.

1

2

3

4

Whirlpool Baths

For those convinced of the healing power of swirling water, the Jacuzzi whirlpool bath may be just the ticket. If you are custom-building a bathroom, you may want to design it around your whirlpool. Some units are exactly the size of a standard tub and can be substituted easily for the one that is in your bathroom now without an expensive remodeling job. For homeowners with more space, there are models with room enough for two.

5

6

7

8

9

10

11

Tubs

There are extra-deep tubs, tubs that accommodate two people, Japanese soaking tubs to use after washing and molded contour tubs, some with seats. Unless you're planning a major remodeling job, most of the more exotic tubs will not fit the dimensions of a standard bathtub area. If you have questions about the practicality of a tub you are considering, ask your local distributor to show you an installation, and discuss the pros and cons with the owner. Some other factors you may want to take into consideration: its length (if you are tall), its depth (if you like to soak up to your chin), and how easy the material is to clean (read manufacturer's brochure for this information).

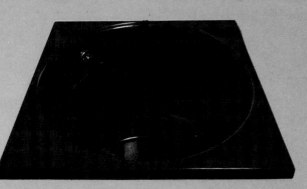

1

2

3

4

5

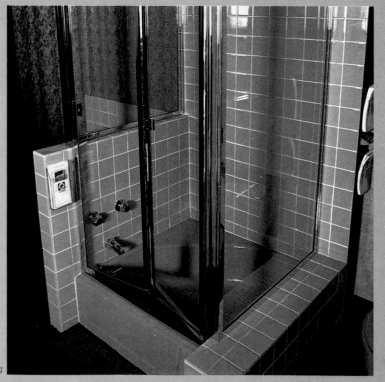

6

Hot Tubs

Redwood hot tubs (7, 8) have become increasingly popular in the last years, especially on the West Coast. Most of us don't have the space for an indoor hot tub, but if you do, the warm water can refresh your body and mind. Hot tubs are a particularly good way to relax after a tense day, but like Japanese soaking tubs, they are not substitutes for a regular bath or shower. Hot tubs may also be constructed outdoors.

7

8

Toilets

Where the water pressure permits, flush valves eliminate the need for a tank behind the toilet to store water until needed for flushing. The newest designs (7, 8, 9) are one-piece and compact, but manufacturers suggest installing them only where water pressure exceeds 15 pounds so the small tanks can be replenished immediately to complete the flushing action. There are specialized toilets designed to fit into corners (6) or to be suspended from the wall so that the floor beneath can be cleaned (not shown). Higher-than-usual toilets can also be installed for the aged or infirm (2). Toilets can match or contrast with the colors of the sink and tub. For help in deciding on bathroom color combinations, see pages 128 and 129. And if you're not sure what your water pressure is, check with the local water department.

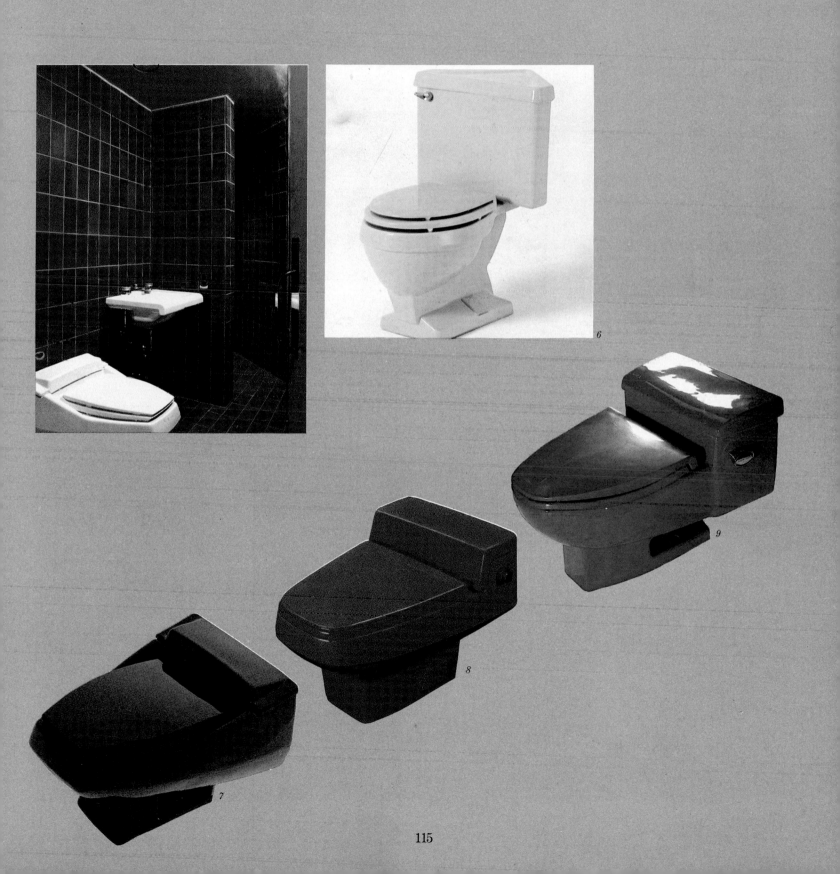

Pedestal Sinks

Besides the wonderful feeling of living with a piece of
sculpture, pedestal sinks do have a practical side. Because
they stand alone, they make small rooms look larger. The idea
goes back to the Victorian era, and some manufacturers are
duplicating the earliest designs (6). For a more current feeling,
there are basins (4,9) that barely touch the wall. If planning a
pedestal for the master bedroom, be sure you have enough
supplemental shelf space for storage. Most pedestals do not
have roomy ledges.

6

7

8

9

Basins

Four pages of basins and we've only begun to show the alternatives. There are several basic types: self-rimming basins, those which require a ring around the perimeter to be attached to the counter, basins mounted under the counter, self-contained units that attach to the wall and require no counter, and Corian molded basin-and-counter combinations (28, 29). In addition to the standard materials, there are beautiful basins of hammered brass, steel, chrome, and

14

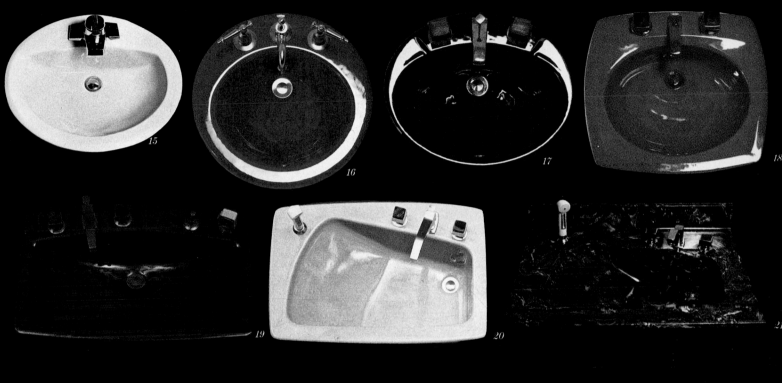

15

16

17

18

19

20

21

22

23

24

25

26

27

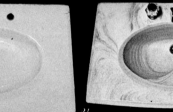

28

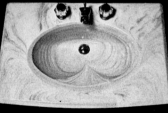

29

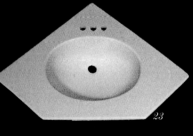

painted porcelain. For people in wheelchairs, there are special
shallow-depth models. Other basins are designed for narrow
counters, small corners and hair-washing with spray
attachments and swing-away spouts (19, 20, page 119). Because
they are usually attached to vanities, basins provide a
fair amount of storage space as well as the convenience of a
long countertop

Bathroom Faucets

You may want to reread the material on kitchen faucets (page 62) since most of the same rules also apply here. A bathroom can be less utilitarian in appearance than a kitchen. Period as well as contemporary designs are available. Some of them are washerless, especially useful for those who are unsure about plumbing repairs.

Faucets are usually mounted in the basin, though some can be mounted in the counter as well.

10

11

12

13

14

15

16

17

18

Color Combinations

Colors shift according to the light, especially pastels. What looks right in the showroom may prove a mismatch when you get it home. All manufacturers offer squares of tile, chips of paint colors, fabric samples and shades of enamel baked onto metal to simulate bath fixtures. It is useful to take these samples back to your bathroom before making a final order. We used them here to suggest combinations of American Standard and Kohler fixture colors with American Olean and Elon tiles and natural stone floors. The plain color samples below show the range of fixture shades available through American Standard and Kohler.

129

Mix and Match Tiles

A series of designs by Sherle Wagner allows you to decide the ultimate pattern of your wall depending on the placement of a set of standard tiles. This is one example of the special custom looks available from some manufacturers. By choosing more than one shade of tile, you can also create special effects with solid tiles. A third alternative is to combine solid and patterned tiles. Careful measuring and graph paper are helpful in making these concepts work.

Towel Rods

The standard towel rod is installed flush with the wall as an integral part of the tiling of the bathroom. Supplementary towel bars come in a vast array of materials and sizes. The old-fashioned solid brass rods have a weight lacking in the modern acrylic and chrome versions. More often than not, the style of the room will be the deciding factor in choosing materials. Some towel ladders provide electrically heated towels, a delicious feeling on a nippy morning. Rods can be affixed to the wall in various ways. Tell your supplier the kind of walls you have before making your final decision on a towel holder.

1

2

3

5

6

7

8

9

10

11

12

13

14

15

16

17

Where space is a problem and a towel bar will not fit, a towel ring will.

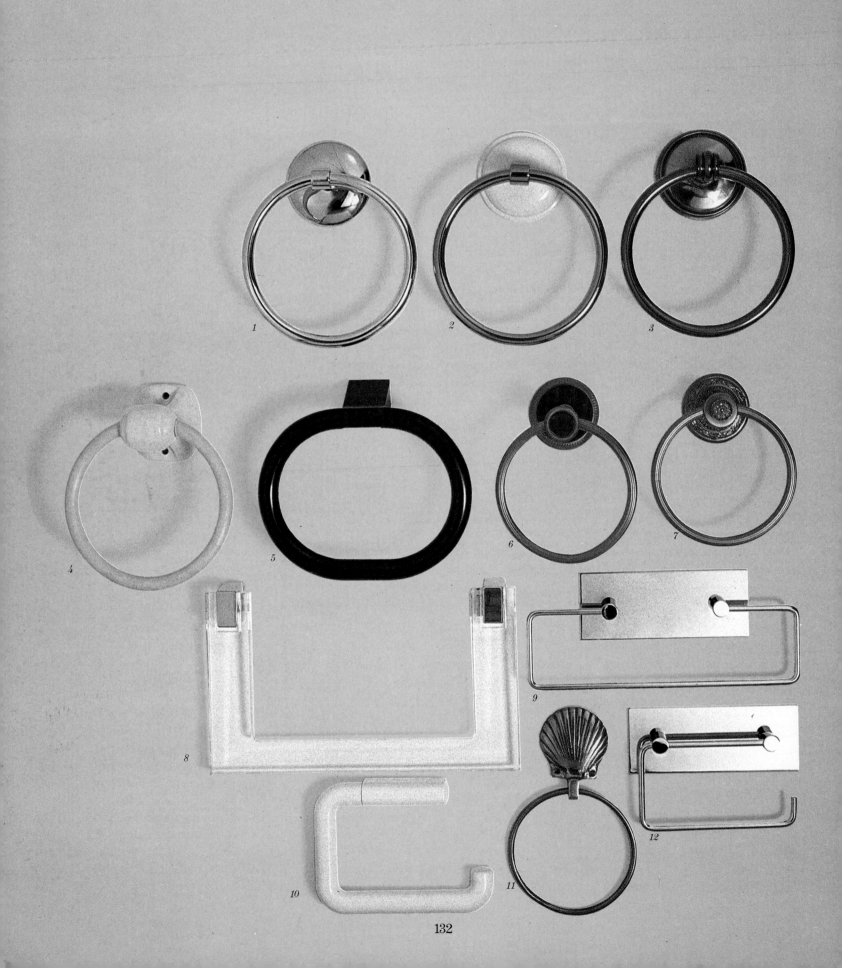

Bath Accessories

The most usual ones are installed as part of the bathroom tile
and become part of the interest of the room. Chrome accessories
by Marchand conceal toilet paper, water glass and tooth brush.

Door Knobs

Interior doors require knobs, but rarely locks and keys. No design job is easier to complete than changing a door knob. The choice depends on the style of the house and your own preferences. For that well-built feeling, nothing beats the heft of a solid brass knob on a solid core door.

1
2
3
4
5
6
7
8
9
10
11
12
13
14
15
16
17

Lever Handles

Originally designed for French windows or narrow passageways
where the hand would rub against the opposite
door if a knob were used, these levers in ceramic, brass and
plastic may suit your similar needs. Lever handles also give a
door a different look and are worth considering for that reason
alone. Many can be opened with the pressure of an elbow,
making them useful for dining room doors, which one often has
to manipulate with a tray full of dishes.

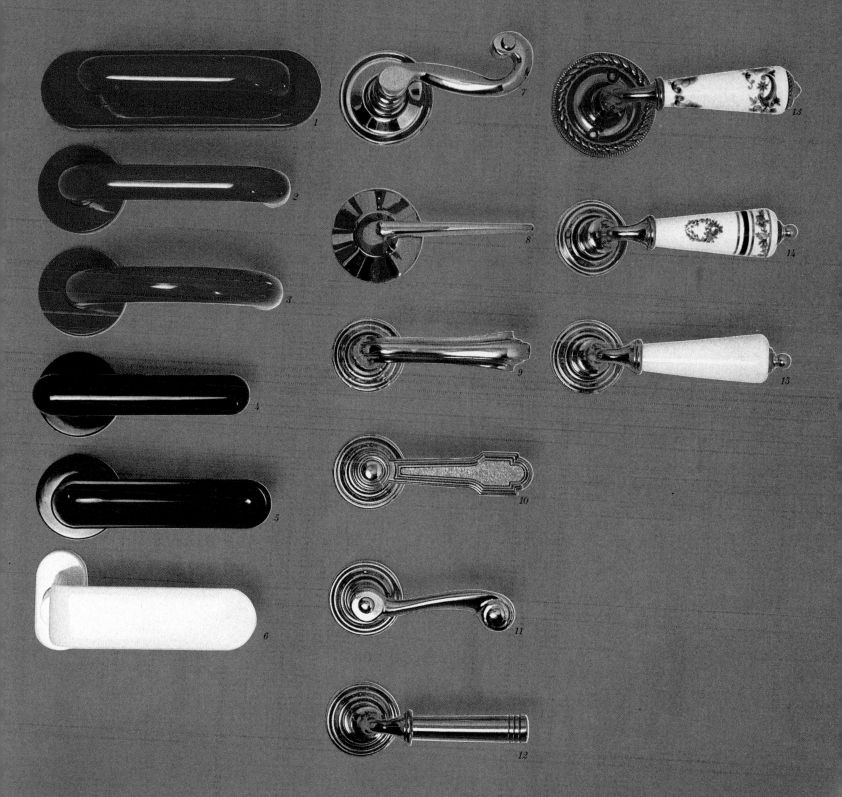

Unusual Hardware

The Ironmonger offers one of the most extensive collections of modern hardware in the United States and imports many of the best products of the European market. Among their offerings are these forearm pulls (1,2,3) from England, which were originally designed for hospitals so that doors could be opened while carrying a heavy tray. Their elegance makes them equally appropriate for a contemporary home setting. The oversize door or cabinet handles (7) come in 10 colors. They are made of solid nylon, with a warmth and smoothness that makes them especially suitable for cold storage room or warm steam baths because their temperature won't fluctuate as much as metal does. The metal hasps (4) are brass. The large center plate can be removed when the fastener is not in use, making it more unobtrusive than the usual hasp. The hasps and the graceful oval handles (5) on this page are from Merit. See page 61 for Ironmonger colors.

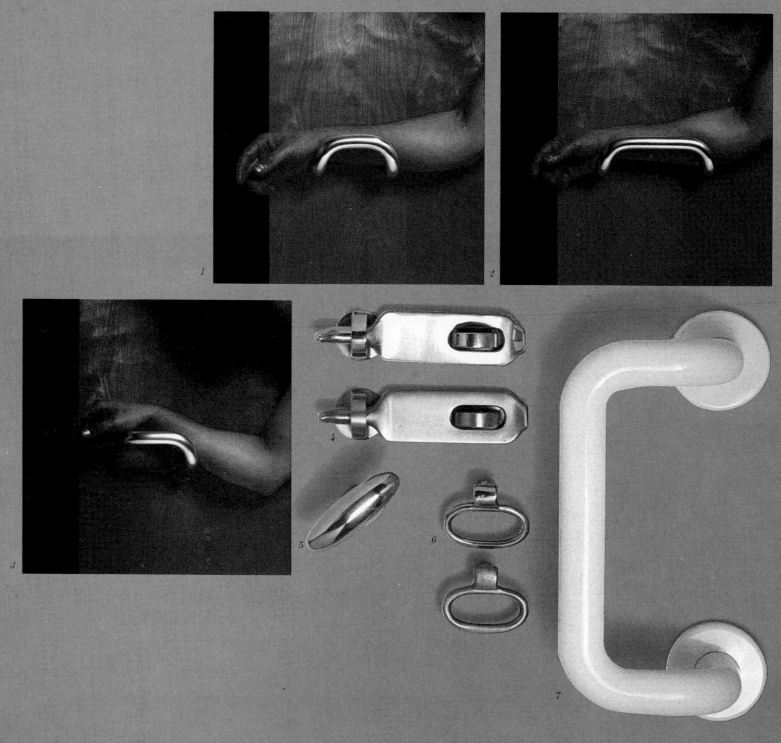

Door Bumpers

Some go on the wall, some on the floor. But wherever they go, bumpers are a way of protecting walls, appliances or fine furniture from bumps and marks that would otherwise be made by the door knob. Door stops are used to hold the door completely (5) or partially open (6). Both these items are examples of the small details that go into a well-planned house.

With only three hours of sunlight a day, you can enjoy year-round gardening with a greenhouse. The simple, inexpensive window units can even be used in an apartment window according to Lord & Burnham, which manufactures a full line. When attaching a greenhouse to your home, a southern, southeastern or southwestern exposure is recommended to capture the maximum amount of November to February sun. The more elaborate greenhouses are worthy of a professional nursery. Among the options available are electric, gas or oil heaters; humidifying equipment; misting systems and thermostats that operate electrically controlled vents.

If you have a door that does not need to be locked or secured with a latch, a classic handle is a handsome way to accessorize it. To get the secure feeling of the door clicking in place, you can install a hidden ball catch at the top of the door which will hold it closed. When having the door painted, be sure to tell the painter not to paint over the ball catch to avoid ruining it.

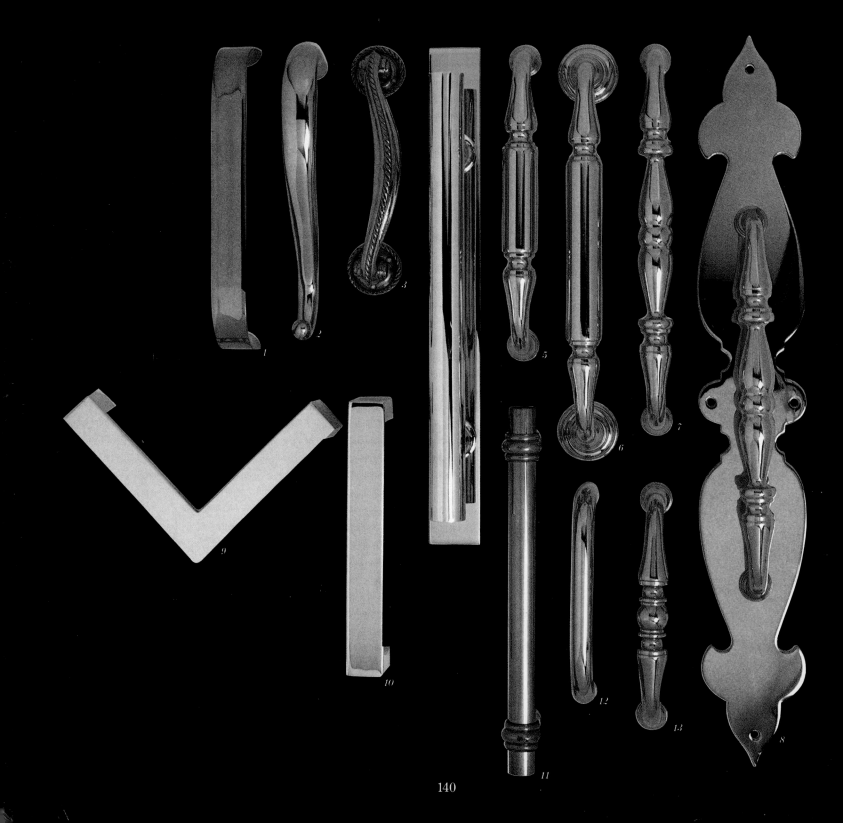

Brass Rim Locks

Originally made in England, these heavy brass units contain the locking mechanism on the rim (face) of the door, rather than mortised into the side of the door (the method by which most contemporary locks operate). Rim locks are as secure as other locks, and they add an authentic touch to traditional houses.

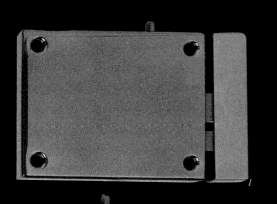

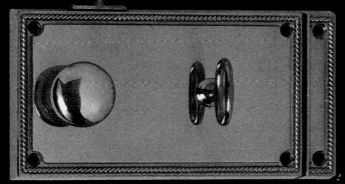

Mortise Locks

For maximum security, mortise locks are preferred to the inexpensive key-in-knob types that are so easy to pick. The attractive handle-and-knob sets shown here are created by Baldwin. They all use the same lock case, which is made of special brass alloys. Those on the opposite page go inside the door, those on this page go outside. The lock cylinder can be chosen from those of many manufacturers. Medeco pickproof cylinders are considered among the best.

Lamp Selector Guide

The **Lamp Selector Guide** and **Lighting Performance Data** on the following pages show the wide range of available lamps —and their lighting performance—that may be used in various fixtures. Lamps are available with narrow, medium and wide beam spreads from 25 watts to 500 watts.

Beam Spread and Footcandles in Center of Beam for 0° aiming angle

Examples

Lamp Selector Guide

A 150 watt PAR-38 Spot lamp at an 8′ mounting distance and a 0° aiming angle will illuminate an area approximately 4′ in diameter and the lighting level in the center of the illuminated area will be 172f.c.

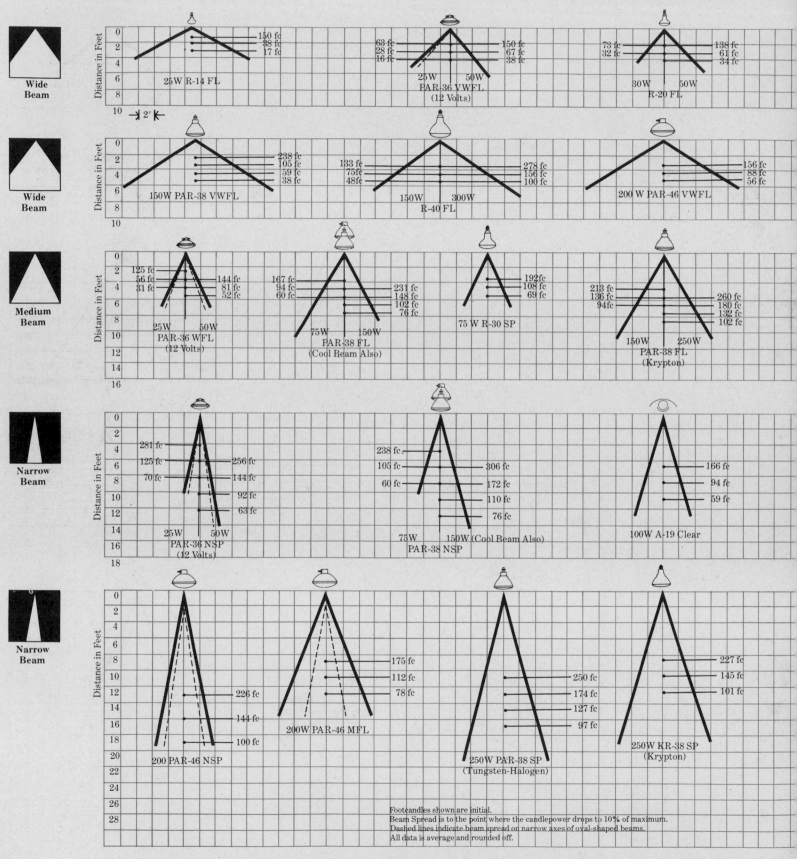

Footcandles shown are initial.
Beam Spread is to the point where the candlepower drops to 10% of maximum.
Dashed lines indicate beam spread on narrow axes of oval-shaped beams.
All data is average and rounded off.

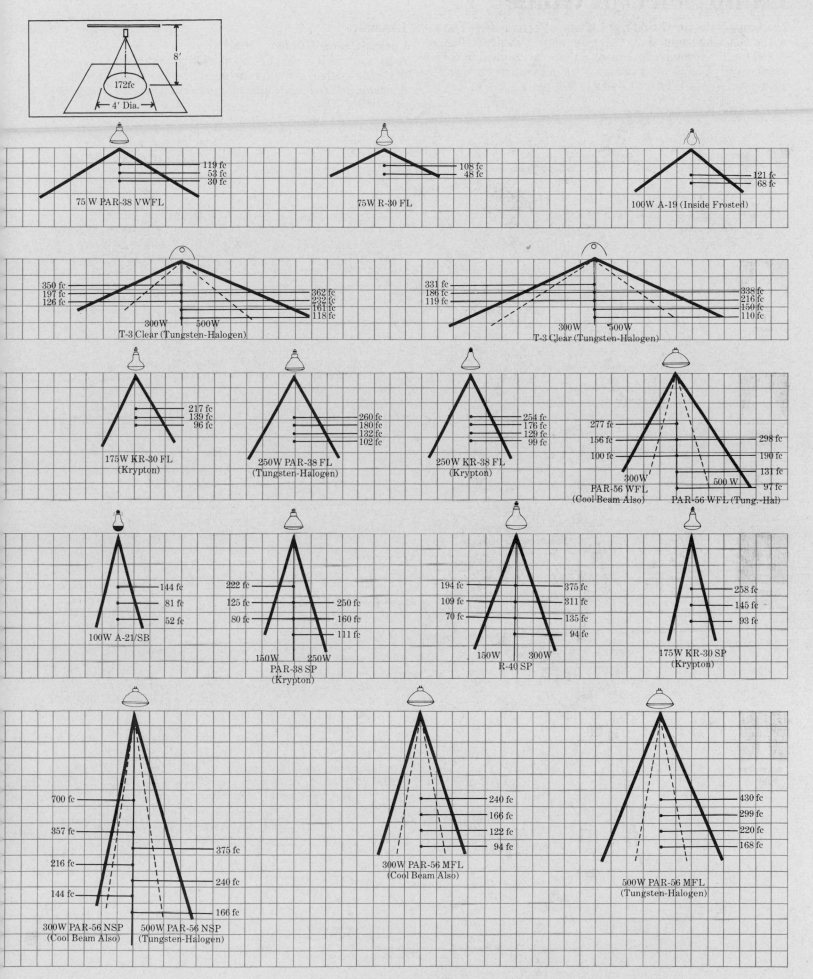

172fc
8'
4' Dia.

75 W PAR-38 VWFL
119 fc
53 fc
30 fc

75W R-30 FL
108 fc
48 fc

100W A-19 (Inside Frosted)
121 fc
68 fc

T-3 Clear (Tungsten-Halogen)
300W   500W
350 fc
197 fc
126 fc
362 fc
232 fc
161 fc
118 fc

T-3 Clear (Tungsten-Halogen)
300W   500W
331 fc
186 fc
119 fc
338 fc
216 fc
150 fc
110 fc

175W KR-30 FL
(Krypton)
217 fc
139 fc
96 fc

250W PAR-38 FL
(Tungsten-Halogen)
260 fc
180 fc
132 fc
102 fc

250W KR-38 FL
(Krypton)
254 fc
176 fc
129 fc
99 fc

PAR-56 WFL
(Cool Beam Also)   PAR-56 WFL (Tung.-Hal)
300W   500 W
277 fc
156 fc
100 fc
298 fc
190 fc
131 fc
97 fc

100W A-21/SB
144 fc
81 fc
52 fc

PAR-38 SP
(Krypton)
150W   250W
222 fc
125 fc
80 fc
250 fc
160 fc
111 fc

R-40 SP
150W   300W
194 fc
109 fc
70 fc
375 fc
311 fc
135 fc
94 fc

175W KR-30 SP
(Krypton)
258 fc
145 fc
93 fc

300W PAR-56 NSP
(Cool Beam Also)   500W PAR-56 NSP
(Tungsten-Halogen)
700 fc
357 fc
216 fc
144 fc
375 fc
240 fc
166 fc

300W PAR-56 MFL
(Cool Beam Also)
240 fc
166 fc
122 fc
94 fc

500W PAR-56 MFL
(Tungsten-Halogen)
430 fc
299 fc
220 fc
168 fc

147

Credits

Pages 18-19
1 Gilt numbers on transom glass.
2,5 Solid brass mail slots.
   Durbin.
3 Solid brass mail slot with
   knocker. *Durbin*.
4 Satin anodized aluminum mail
   slot. *The Ironmonger*.
6 Solid brass interior mail slot.
   The Heritage Collection.
7 Solid brass mail slot with flap.
   Period Furniture Hardware.

Pages 20-21
1 Helvetica molded weatherproof
   foam numbers can be painted
   the color of your choice.
   The Ironmonger.
2,8 Solid brass numbers.
   Custom Decor.
3 Helvetica self-adhesive vinyl
   numbers in a range of sizes in
   black or white. *Letraset*.
4 El Boldo molded weatherproof
   foam numbers to be painted any
   color. *The Ironmonger*.
5 Brass numbers from India
   courtesy of *Placewares*.
6 Brass numbers.
   Safe Hardware.
7 Enamel number plaques from
   England courtesy of *Conran's*.
9 Solid brass numbers.
   Durbin.

Pages 22-23
1 Oversized solid brass lion head
   knocker.
   Period Furniture Hardware.
2 Solid brass pendant knocker.
   The Heritage Collection.
3 Black wrought iron colonial
   knocker.
   The Heritage Collection.
4,5 Five solid brass ring knockers
   courtesy of *William A. Hunrath*
6 Solid brass fox head knocker.
   Custom Décor.
7 Solid brass dog head knocker.
   Custom Décor.
8 Solid brass dolphin knocker.
   Custom Décor.
9 Traditional brass oval knocker
   Period Furniture Hardware.
10 Modern brass knocker
   courtesy of *William A. Hunrath*
11 Solid brass pendant knocker.
   Custom Décor.
12 Solid brass ring knocker.
   The Heritage Collection.
13 Satin anodized aluminum
   knocker. *The Ironmonger*.
14 Solid brass pineapple knocker.
   Period Furniture Hardware.

Pages 24-25
Entrance doors in a variety of
designs for traditional or
contemporary homes in wood or
insulated galvanized steel.
Wood doors: *C.E. Morgan*.
Steel doors: *Steelcraft*.
Range of pre-painted colors for
steel doors: *Steelcraft*.

Page 27
Interior wood doors in a range of
styles and sizes. *C.E. Morgan*.

Pages 28-29
1 Colonial strap hinge courtesy of
   William A. Hunrath.
2 Solid brass strap hinge.
   Custom Décor.
3,5 Solid brass hinges.
   Merit Metal Products.
4 Decorative gold-plated hinge.
   Sherle Wagner.
6 Solid brass hinge courtesy of
   Paine & Chriscot.
7 Solid brass hinge courtesy of
   William A. Hunrath.
8,9,11 Solid brass hinges.
   Period Furniture Hardware.
10 Soss invisible hinge courtesy of
   William A. Hunrath.

Pages 30-31
1 Unbreakable nylon single
   ceiling hook.
   The Ironmonger.
2 Unbreakable nylon rotating
   skyhook. *The Ironmonger*.
3 Plastic swivel ceiling hook.
   IDG.
4,13 Plastic hooks.
   IDG.
5,6 Unbreakable nylon hooks.
   The Ironmonger.
7 Jumbo plastic hook.
   IDG.
8 Quadruple plastic hook.
   IDG.
9 Ceramic hooks.
   Ajax Hardware.
10 Double hook in wood courtesy of
   Conran's.
11 Hat and coat hook.
   The Ironmonger.

12 Cylindrical knob hook.
The Ironmonger.
14 Single hook in unbreakable
nylon. *The Ironmonger.*
15,16,17 Plastic hat and coat hooks.
IDG.
18,19 Decorative gold-plated and
porcelain hooks.
Sherle Wagner.
20 Decorative gold-plated and
Tiger Eye hook.
Sherle Wagner.
21 Brass hook courtesy of
Paine & Chriscot.
22 Brass shell hook.
Custom Décor.
23-30 Classic hooks in chrome and
brass courtesy of
William A. Hunrath.
31 Pull-out hook courtesy of
William A. Hunrath.
32 Solid brass swing hook.
Custom Décor.
33 Black wrought iron hook
courtesy of
William A. Hunrath.
34 Cylindrical chrome mini-hooks.
The Ironmonger.
35 Soft, tough, resilient neoprene
hook with metal backing from
Forms and Surfaces,
courtesy of *Placewares.*
36 Satin anodized aluminum hook.
The Ironmonger.
37 Solid brass single hook.
Custom Décor.
38 Brass hat and coat hook.
Unique Handicrafts.

Pages 34-35
1,3 Quarry tile in a range of colors
and shapes. *American Olean.*
2 Primitive tile, glazed and
unglazed, in a range of colors,
sizes. *American Olean.*
4 Glazed handmade Mexican tile.
Elon.

Pages 36-37
Granite (1), Belgian stone (2),
and slate (3), courtesy of the
Building Stone Institute.

Pages 38-39
1 Wood flooring in an extensive
range of patterns, woods.
Hoboken Wood Flooring.

2 Dura-seal wood stains (on red
oak flooring).
Minwax Company.
3 GenuWood, a bonding of wood
veneer and vinyl, in a range of
woods. Also available in cork.
PermaGrain Products.

Page 40
Dennis Mortensen, architect.

Pages 42-43
1 Olson/Walker Associates,
architects.
2 Dwyer and Dwyer, designers.
3 Robert Mabry/Royce La Nier,
architects.

Pages 46-47
Kitchen plans courtesy of
Poggenpohl USA.

Page 48
Designalliance (J. Paul Gainey).

Page 49
1 Electric surface range.
Chambers.
2 Electric cooktop. *Tappan.*
3 Electric cooktop with small
auxiliary burner. *Thermador.*
4 Gas cooktop. *Tappan.*
5 Electric cooktop. *Tappan.*
6,8 Stainless steel electric cooktop
with grill/griddle. Shown open
and closed. *Thermador.*
7 Gas cooktop with electric
ignition system. *Chambers.*

Pages 50-51
1 Andrew Scallan/Bernardo
Rostad, architects.

Alpes-Inox stainless steel
cooktops.
2 Corner unit with gas and
electric burners plus grill.
3 Four single units installed as one
allow flexibility in planning.
Shown here are a combination of
electric and gas burners and
grills.
4 Large six-burner gas unit with
grill.
5 Large six-burner unit
combining gas and electric
burners. *Kamenow.*

Page 52
1 Three-section convertible grill-
range. Can be arranged with
double grill or double cooktop.
Grill can be replaced with
griddle. *Jenn-Air.*
2 Single, non-convertible grill.
Jenn-Air.
Accessories for Jenn-Air grills.
3 Rotisserie.
4 Griddle with non-stick surface.
5 Rotisserie cover.
6 French fryer with basket and
temperature gauge.
7 Four-skewer shish-kebob.

Page 53
William F. Creager, designer.

Pages 56-57
1 Party sink with gooseneck
pantry faucet.
American Standard.
2 Enameled cast-iron double-bowl
sink. *American Standard.*
3 Enameled cast-iron single-bowl
sink. *American Standard.*
4 Compact enameled cast-iron
single-bowl sink with corner
disposal. *Kohler.*
5,8 Enameled cast-iron double-
bowl sink with raised basin for
disposal, large bowl for pots and
pans. Optional cutting board.
Kohler.

6 Party sink with cutting board,
stainless steel garnish cups.
Kohler.
7 Enameled cast-iron triple-bowl
sink with center disposal,
optional drainboard and cutting
board. *Kohler.*
9 Alape two-bowl sink of vitreous
enamel-covered steel shown
with drain basket.
Architectural Complements.

Pages 58-59
1 Space-saving curved corner
double-bowl sink.
American Standard.
2 Bar sink with NuTone blender
unit. *Elkay.*
3 Triple-bowl sink with NuTone
blender unit. Small bowl can be
used as bar sink. *Just.*

Pages 80-81

1-7 Enamel-coated or chrome cast Zemak pulls. *Ajax Hardware.*

8-12 Plastic pulls. *Ajax Hardware.*

13-16 Plastic pulls in six colors. *Omnia.*

17-18 Chip-resistant pulls in seven colors. *Omnia.*

19-21 Plastic pulls in six colors. *Omnia.*

22-27 Extruded aluminum pulls in a variety of finishes. *Epco.*

28-32 Off-set pulls in five finishes. *Epco.*

33-36 Wire pulls in two sizes, chrome or brass. *Omnia.*

37-39 Plastic U-pulls in six colors. *Omnia.*

40-41 U-pulls in brass and chrome. *Omnia.*

42 White nylon U-pull courtesy of *Placewares.*

43 Transparent plastic pull from *Forms & Surfaces* courtesy of *Placewares.*

44 Red plastic pull. *IDG.*

45-50 Unbreakable nylon pulls in ten colors, a variety of shapes and sizes. *The Ironmonger.*

51 Recessed pull in matte nickle (also polished brass). *The Ironmonger.*

52 Recessed plastic pull courtesy of *Placewares.*

53,54 Recessed unfinished wood pulls from *Forms & Surfaces* courtesy of *Placewares.*

55 Chrome pull courtesy of *William A. Hunrath.*

56,57 Adjustable length brass and plastic pulls in a variety of colors and sizes courtesy of *Paine & Chriscot.*

58-65 Chrome and brass pulls. *Omnia.*

66 Recessed brass pull courtesy of *Paine & Chriscot.*

67 Traditional brass pull. *Custom Décor.*

68 Decorative gold-plated pull. *Sherle Wagner.*

69-70 Double wire pulls in two sizes, brass or chrome. *Omnia.*

71-72 Brass or chrome pulls, two sizes. *Omnia.*

73-74 Classic cast brass pulls, polished or brushed finish. *Merit Metal Products.*

75-76 Traditional solid brass pulls. *Custom Décor.*

77-79 Porcelain pulls in two sizes, three shapes, six colors. *Trend Pacific.*

80-84 Soft knobs of tough, resilient neoprene in a variety of shapes from *Forms & Surfaces* courtesy of *Placewares.*

85 Plastic draw pull. *IDG.*

Pages 82-83

1-4 Plastic knobs in a range of colors. *Ajax Hardware.*

5-7 Chip-resistant ball knobs in two sizes, four colors. *Omnia.*

8-15 Convex knobs in a range of sizes, colors. *Omnia.*

16, 17 Plastic knobs courtesy of *Placewares.*

18-20 Plastic knobs in three sizes, five colors. *IDG.*

21 Large nylon knob in a range of ten colors. *The Ironmonger.*

22 Satin chrome knob. *The Ironmonger.*

23-28 Soft knobs of tough, resilient neoprene from *Forms & Surfaces* courtesy of *Placewares.*

29 Brass knob. *Baldwin.*

30-32 Brass or chrome knobs in three sizes. *Omnia.*

33-34 Ball knobs in chrome or brass. *Omnia.*

35-37 Satin chrome ball knobs. *The Ironmonger.*

38,39 Decorative gold-plated knobs. *Sherle Wagner.*

40 Satin chrome knob. *The Ironmonger.*

41-43 Cylindrical pulls in polished brass or chrome in three sizes. *Omnia.*

44 Brass pull inset with teak. *Stanley Hardware.*

45-47 Square unfinished wood knobs in three sizes. *Belwith.*

48,49 Unfinished hardwood knobs in two sizes. *Belwith.*

50,51 Unfinished wood knobs from *Forms & Surfaces* courtesy of *Placewares.*

52-53 Unfinished wood ball knobs in four sizes. *Belwith.*

54-56 Convex unfinished wood knobs in four sizes. *Belwith.*

57,58 Flat knobs in unfinished wood. *Belwith.*

59-63 Ceramic knobs in a range of colors. *Ajax Hardware.*

64,65 Porcelain knobs in two sizes. *Belwith.*

66-73 Colonial porcelain knobs in a complete range of sizes. *Belwith.*

74 Porcelain knob in three sizes, six colors. *Trend Pacific.*

75-76 Porcelain knobs. *Belwith.*

77-78 Decorative Limoges porcelain knobs. *Baldwin.*

79-80 Decorative porcelain knobs in several sizes and designs. *The Heritage Collection.*

81-83 Porcelain ball knobs in three sizes. *Belwith.*

84 Decorative porcelain knob. *Belwith.*

85 "Crackled" ceramic knob. *Ajax Hardware.*

Page 84

Robert Mabry/Royce La Nier, architects.

Rugs and antiques courtesy of *Trocadero Arts of Man,* Washington, D.C.

Pages 114-115

1 European-styled toilet. *American Standard*, courtesy of *Smolka*.
2 Extra-height toilet for the elderly and infirm. *Kohler*.
3 Classic, elongated Cadet toilet. *American Standard*, courtesy of *Smolka*.
4 Modern toilet from Italy in 25 color combinations. *Hastings*.
5 Italian toilet with fluted exterior, white interior. *Hastings*.
6 Space-saving corner toilet, *Eljer*.
7 Low-silhouette, no-overflow toilet. *Kohler*.
8 Clean-lined, one-piece toilet with unique waterfall tank cover. *Eljer*.
9 Contemporary, one-piece styling. *American Standard*, courtesy of *Smolka*.

Pages 116-117

1 Traditional porcelain pedestal sink. *The Heritage Collection*.
2 European-styled lavatory. *American Standard*, courtesy of *Smolka*.
3 Contemporary pedestal lavatory *American Standard*, courtesy of *Smolka*.
4 Italian pedestal sink in 25 color combinations. *Hastings*.
5 Fluted Italian pedestal sink with white interior. *Hastings*.

6 China pedestal washstand. *Sherle Wagner*.
7 Wide-rimmed contemporary pedestal sink. *Eljer*.
8 Structurally shaped Italian pedestal sink. *Hastings*.
9 Graceful large-basin pedestal sink, melding American design and European styling. *Kohler*.

Pages 118-119

1 White porcelain basin, also available decorated. *The Heritage Collection*.
2 Handmade terra-cotta basin from Mexico. *Elon*.
3 Wide-rimmed chrome basin. *Paul Associates*.
4 Alape enamel lavatory. *Architectural Complements*.
5 Chrome-rimmed lavatory for narrow counter installations. *American Standard*.
6,7,8 Enameled lavatories in choice of sizes, styles. *American Standard*.
9 Handcarved and polished marble basin. *Sherle Wagner*.
10 Alape wall-hung enamel sink. *Architectural Complements*.
11 Polished brass basin. *Piazza Faucets*.
12 Hammered chrome basin. *Piazza Faucets*.
13 Vitreous china lavatory for counter installations. *Kohler*.
14 Wall-hung lavatory for small spaces. *American Standard*.
15 Self-rimmed lavatory. *American Standard*.
16-18 Self-rimmed lavatories. *Kohler*.

19 Deep basin lavatory designed especially for men. Shampoo spray, soap-lotion dispenser, swing spout. *Kohler*.
20 Self-rimmed lavatory shaped for shampooing, bathing the baby. Shampoo spray, swing spout. *Kohler*.
21 Marble shampoo basin with retractable spray, swing spout. *Westchester Venetian Marble*.
22 Wall-hung corner sink for small spaces. *Eljer*.
23 Corner lavatory of DuPont Corian® courtesy of *Salisbury Sales*.
24 Luxurious wide-rimmed lavatory. *American Standard*.
25 Marble china wide-ledged lavatory. *American Standard*.
26,27 Self-rimmed lavatories. *Eljer*.
28,29 Single and double molded DuPont Corian® lavatories in any length. *Salisbury Sales*.

Pages 120-121

1 Decorative white porcelain basin. *Sherle Wagner*.
2 Brushed platinum decorative basin. *Sherle Wagner*.
3-5 Decorative porcelain basins. *Sherle Wagner*.
6 Sculpted white marble lavatory. *Westchester Venetian Marble*.
7 European wall-hung scallop-shaped lavatory in marble china. *American Standard*, courtesy of *Smolka*.
8 Ground marble/resin blend molded into a vanity top with shell-shaped basin. *Molded Marble Products*.
9 Sculptured shell lavatory in Mexican onyx. *Westchester Venetian Marble*.
10 Sculpted brass basin. *Smolka*.
11-15 Decorated porcelain basins. *Sherle Wagner*.
16,17 Hand-made and hand-decorated basins from Mexico. *Elon*.
18,19 Decorated porcelain basins. *Sherle Wagner*.
20 Hand-carved and polished marble basin. *Sherle Wagner*.
21 White marble vanity top with decorated porcelain basin. *Sherle Wagner*.

Page 134

1 Drop pull in solid brass. *Baldwin.*
2 Gold plated decorative knob. *Sherle Wagner.*
3 Decorative Limoges porcelain knob. *Baldwin.*
4 Nylon knob in ten colors. *The Ironmonger.*
5 Decorative brass knob courtesy of *Paine & Chriscot.*
6 Solid brass oval knob. *Baldwin.*
7 Cut Lucite knob courtesy of *William A. Hunrath.*
8 White nylon oval knob. *Baldwin.*
9 Traditional forged brass knob. *Baldwin.*
10 Solid brass knob. *Baldwin.*
11 Decorative oval brass knob courtesy of *Paine & Chriscot.*
12 Faceted solid brass knob. *Durbin.*
13 Solid brass oval knob courtesy of *William A. Hunrath.*
14 Satin anodized aluminum knob. *The Ironmonger.*
15,17 Solid brass knobs. *Baldwin.*
16 White Limoges porcelain knob. *Baldwin.*

Page 135

1-3 Nylon lever handles in three shapes, ten colors. *The Ironmonger.*
4-6 Italian-designed plastic lever handles in three shapes, five colors. *The Ironmonger.*
7,9,10,11 Solid brass lever handles. *Baldwin.*
8 Solid brass lever handle courtesy of *William A. Hunrath.*
12 Solid brass lever handle. *Baldwin.*
13 Decorated porcelain lever handle. *The Heritage Collection.*
14 Decorated Limoges porcelain lever handle. *Baldwin.*
15 Limoges porcelain lever handle. *Baldwin.*

Page 136

1,2,3 Limbar forearm doorpulls in satin anodized aluminum. *The Ironmonger.*
4 Hasp closure in polished or brushed brass. *Merit Metal Products.*
5 Tee handle in polished brass. *Merit Metal Products.*
6 Drop handle in polished or brushed brass. *Merit Metal Products.*
7 Offset nylon doorpull in ten colors. *The Ironmonger.*

Page 137

1 Nylon and rubber doorstop. *The Ironmonger.*
2 Brass and rubber doorstop, courtesy of *Paine & Chriscot.*
3,4 Large and small satin anodized|aluminum and rubber doorstops. *The Ironmonger.*
5,6 Brass doorholders. *Safe.*
7,8 Nylon/rubber door bumpers in ten colors. *The Ironmonger.*
9,10 Rubber-tipped brass door bumpers. *Safe.*
11 Satin anodized aluminum and rubber door bumper. *The Ironmonger.*

Pages 138-139

Stock and custom-designed greenhouses by *Lord & Burnham.*

Page 140

1,2,5,6,7,8,12,13 Solid brass door pulls. *Baldwin.*
3 Decorative brass door pull. *Durbin.*
4 Heavy-duty chrome door pull courtesy of *William A. Hunrath.*
9 Satin anodized aluminum door pull. *The Ironmonger.*
10 Chrome door pull courtesy of *William A. Hunrath.*
11 Adjustable length brass door pull courtesy of *Paine & Chriscot.*

Page 141

1,3 Solid brass rim locks. *Baldwin.*
2 Decorative rim lock. *The Heritage Collection.*
4 Brass rim lock. *Merit.*

Pages 142-143

1 Manhattan polished chrome square-knobbed interior trim.
2 Boston polished brass interior trim.
3 Hyde Park polished brass lever handle interior trim.
4 Dallas polished chrome lever handle interior trim.
5 Chicago polished chrome interior trim.
6 Lexington dull brass and brown interior trim.
7 Richmond oil-rubbed bronze interior trim.
8 Portsmouth polished brass lever handle interior trim.
9 Richmond exterior lock trim.
10 Lexington exterior lock trim.
11 Chicago exterior lock trim.
12 Dallas exterior lock trim.
13 Polished brass exterior lock trim.
14 Hyde Park exterior lock trim.
15 Boston exterior lock trim.
16 Manhattan exterior lock trim.
17 Portsmouth exterior lock trim.
All lock trim from *Baldwin.*

Index of Manufacturers

Driwood Moulding Co.
P.O. Box 1729
Florence, SC 29503

E.I. DuPont de Nemours & Co.,
Inc.
Wilmington, DE 19898

Durbin Industries, Inc.
1434 Woodson Road
St. Louis, MO 63132

Dwyer Products Corp.
Michigan City, IN 46360

Eljer Plumbingwear Division
Three Gateway Center
Pittsburgh, PA 15222

Elkay Manufacturing Co.
2700 S. 17th Avenue
Broadview, IL 60153

Elon, Inc.
198 Saw Mill River Road
Elmsford, NY 10523

Epco
Engineered Products Co.
601 Kelso Street
P.O. Box 108
Flint, MI 48501

Euro-Concepts Ltd.
150 East 58th Street
New York, NY 10022
(custom kitchens)

Evans Clay Products, Inc.
Midvale, OH 44653

Formica
Division of American Cyanamid
120 E. Fourth Street
Cincinnati, OH 45202

Forms & Surfaces
Box 5215
Santa Barbara, CA 93108

General Electric
Appliance Park
Louisville, KY 40229

Georgia-Pacific
900 S.W. Fifth Avenue
Portland, OR 97204

Go-Met-Tile Associates, Inc.
979 Third Avenue
New York, NY 10022

Also:
351 Peachtree Hills
Avenue NE
Atlanta, GA 30305

Great North Woods
683 Lexington Avenue
New York, NY 10022

Harris Manufacturing Co.
734 E. Walnut Street
Johnson City, TN 37601
(wood flooring)

Hastings Tile, Il Bagno Collection
964 Third Avenue
New York, NY 10022

H.C. Products Co.
Princeville, IL 61559
(shutters, folding doors)

Heatilator
Division of Vega Industries
Mt. Pleasant, IA 52641

Heritage Collection
Division of Broadway Supply Co.
250 N. Troost Street
Olathe, KS 66061

Hoboken Wood Flooring
100 Willow Street
East Rutherford, NJ 07073

William A. Hunrath
153 E. 57th Street
New York, NY 10022
(retail decorative hardware)

ICF Inc.
145 E. 57th Street
New York, NY 10022

IDG Marketing Ltd.
1100 Slocum Avenue
Ridgefield, NJ 07657

The Ironmonger
1822 N. Sheffield
Chicago, IL 60614
(through architects only)

Ives
P.O. Box 1887
Ives Place
New Haven, CT 06508

Jacuzzi
298 N. Wiget Lane
P.O. Drawer J
Walnut Creek, CA 94596

Jenn-Air
3035 Shadeland Avenue
Indianapolis, IN 46226

Just Manufacturing Co.
9233 King Street
Franklin Park, IL 60131

Kamenow, Inc.
250 E. 52nd Street
New York, NY 10022

Kentile Floors, Inc.
979 Third Avenue
New York, NY 10022

Kentucky Wood Floors
7761 National Turnpike
Louisville, KY 40214

Kinkead Industries, Inc.
2801 Finley Road
Downers Grove, IL 60515
(tub-shower enclosures, doors)

Kohler Co.
Kohler, WI 53044

Lake Shore Industries
2806 N. Reynolds Road
Toledo, OH 43615
(doors)

Letraset
483 Tenth Avenue
New York, New York 10018

Lido International
150 E. 58th Street
New York, NY 10022

Lighting Services
150 E. 58th Street
New York, NY 10022
(track lighting)

Lightolier
346 Claremont Avenue
Jersey City, NJ 07305

Lord & Burnham
Irvington-on-Hudson, NY 10533

Manhattan Ad Hoc
842 Lexington Avenue
New York, NY 10021
(retail housewares store)

A. Marchand Inc.
Southampton, PA 18966

Medeco Locks
P.O. Box 1075
Salem, VA 24153

Merit Metal Products Corp.
242 Valley Road
Warrington, PA 18976

Metropolitan Wire
Wilkes-Barre, PA 18703

Minwax Co., Inc.
Clifton, NJ 07014

Moen
Division of Stanadyne
377 Woodland Avenue
Elyria, OH 44035

Molded Marble Products
Division of Lippert Corp.
P.O. Box 219
W142 N8999 Fountain Blvd.
Menomonee Falls, WI 53051

C.E. Morgan
P.O. Box 2446
601 Oregon Street
Oshkosh, WI 54903

Mylen Industries, Inc.
650 Washington Street
Peekskill, NY 10566

Norco Sash and Door Co.
Hawkins, WI 54530

NuTone
Division of Scovill
Madison & Red Bank Roads
Cincinnati, OH 45227
(Blender units, in-wall vacuum
outlets, intercom systems)

NuVu Window-Insulation Co.
15555 C. S. Frederick Road
Rockville, MD 20855

Old World Moulding & Finishing,
Inc.
115 Allen Blvd.
Farmingdale, NY

Omnia Industries, Inc.
P.O. Box 263
49 Park Street
Montclair, NJ 07042

Paine & Chriscot
1187 Second Avenue
New York, NY 10021
(retail decorative hardware)

Charles Parker
290 Pratt Street
Meriden, CT 06450
(commercial bathroom accessories)

S. Parker Hardware
27 Ludlow Street
New York, NY 10022

Paul Associates
155 E. 55th Street
New York, NY 10022

Period Furniture Hardware Co.,
Inc.
P.O. Box 314
Charles Street Station
123 Charles Street
Boston, MA 02114

PermaGrain Products, Inc.
22 West State Street
Suite 302
Media, PA 19063

Piazza Faucets, Inc.
6911 Younger Drive
Buena Park, CA 90620

Placewears
13 Walden Street
Concord, MA 01742
(retail store)

Poggenpohl USA
222 Cedar Lane
Teaneck, NJ 07666

Potlatch Corp. (Townsend Wood
Wall Planks)
P.O. Box 916
Stuttgart, AR 72160

Powers-Fiat Corp.
3400 Oakton Street
Skokie, IL 60076

Peter Reimuller,
The Greenhouseman
Santa Cruz, CA 95062
980 First Avenue

Rodac Corp.
P.O. Box 5247
1005 E. Astoria Blvd.
Carson, CA 90746

Roper Sales Corp.
Kankakee, IL 60901
(ranges and cooktops)

Safe Hardware Corp.
225 Episcopal Road
Berlin, CT 06037

St. Charles Fashion Kitchens
St. Charles, IL 60174

Salisbury Sales Co., Inc.
140 Atlantic Street
Hackensack, NJ 07601

Salvarani
(see Lido)

Schlage Lock Co.
Bayshore Boulevard
P.O. Box 3324
San Francisco, CA 94119

Sherle Wagner
60 E. 57th Street
New York, NY 10022

Smolka Co.
233 E. 33rd Street
New York, NY 10001

Soss Manufacturing Co.
21777 Hoover Road
Warren, MI 48089